MARATHON RUNNER

SURVIVING THE ISSUES OF LIFE

By Carolyn Woodland

Restored
Copyright © 2016 Carolyn Woodland

ISBN: 978-1-938950-69-8

Greater is He Publishing
9824 E. Washington St,
Chagrin Falls Ohio 44023
P O. Box 39283 Solon Ohio, 44139

Dedication

I would like to dedicate this book to anyone out there who has been through something and maybe still going though some things. I would like to encourage you to keep on pushing on, no matter what happens in your life. Take time to pray; god has taken time to listen. There will come a time in your life when you have to choose to turn the page of a chapter in your life or close the book and allow the lord to rewrite you another one. God's timing is always perfect. He is never too early or too late. With every passing moment of your life, he is there to bless you and fill you with his undying love, so give your life to him and live.

Contents

ACKNOWLEDGMENTS:

I give honor to God who is the head of my life and the lover of my soul and my strength, my guiding light, my all in all, my everything and more. To my late mother, Alice R. Espay, you were such an awesome mother to me. I thank you so much for all the hard work you put into providing the love that nurtured me because that was very critical for all my accomplishments, for my encouragement and for all the immeasurable love I have, resting in God's arms.

To my loving father, Andrew Espay, a very awesome, strong father who knew what the word "father" was all about. He was my daddy and a true Godsend to this world. He was an awesome singer and preacher as well as a great dad, resting in Gods arms.

To the four young men in my life who love me for me and want nothing but the best, I thank God for them always. These young men have come up in life with prayers; to look at them is to see the wonders of God. Love you, Frank, Eugene, Rayshawn, and Brandon, my sons.

I would also like to thank a loving and caring friend, Ms. Carolyn Wanzo. This woman has been with me through thick and thin. She prays for me and listens to my every word, right or wrong. When God puts someone in your life that cares and prays for you and you for them, it's real. Don't misuse it, ever. God sure will put people in your life to push you.

And to all my loving and caring nieces and nephews, God has a plan for your lives. Just stay strong in the Lord, keep pushing on (I'm just saying).

To my loving sister, Lisa, and my brothers, Ricky and Michael. Keep looking up to heaven. God hears you. Never let go. Love you all!!! Be Blessed in all that you do.

To Greater is He Publishing Co, thank you. Especially to all the loving and caring people of your publishing team for their delicate handling, their patience and their God-given vision for everything they do, I thank you.

Ms. Woodland

Chapter 1 –
A True Marathon Running

Have you ever considered yourself to be a marathon runner? Are you running a hundred miles in the wrong direction through life, taking care of business trying to survive the storms of life? Or is your strength gone from you? Maybe you need to put that on a critical list. You have never really lived and survived until you have done some things, been through some things, and survived, or until you've done something for someone besides yourself who can never repay you back. Have you truly been through the storms of life? Are you a true marathon runner? I bet you are; just think about it. You are running through this world doing all sorts of things for everybody, family, friends, your spouse, your children, even your job. And if you are a single parent raising children alone, you still are a marathon runner — and you thought it was going to be easy, those little hands, ten toes, ten fingers, a beautiful smile, and not a care in the world. All they need is your attention and your love, in spite of what's going on around them. Tell me if you can relate to this or not.

Were you one of those people who got to this point the wrong way, you know, not Gods way? One late night out with the love of your life, you thought. You were doing all the things you were supposed to be doing: living right, reading God's word, working, going to school and most of all keeping yourself until marriage. You know the things God talks about in His word. The things we were taught when we were growing up as children. But all of a sudden, you decided to test the waters a little and just give the love of your life a little sample of your goods. Did you say this to him or her: "Let me show you what I'm working with"? Let's keep it real people, but keep it clean. If you are reading this book and life has thrown you for a loop, and you are barely hanging on, don't worry. God is here to help you, so let's finish the story.

A Finished Conversation:

It was late one night and the stars were out—a nice summer night—and you should have taken your behind home, but you said, "I got this. I can handle it. God's got me." You see how that went? We always put God where He did not ask to be. We always allow God to step out of the picture while we do our dirt. He didn't ask to be in stuff He has tried to keep us from. We all know exactly what we are doing; you would think we would have full control over it, but we really don't. Here you go, the start of your marathon, allowing your head and your body to take control of your mind. Now let's see where this takes you. It is too late; you can't go back. The deed is done — yes, the act of sex and all that comes with it, without the blessing of God, without marriage. WOW!! You think you just ran a race, that your marathon is just beginning; no, this is the beginning of the rest of your life. You don't even have time to stop and breathe yet. You fix yourself up, take a deep breath and say goodnight. You leave with so much running in your mind. What's next? You ask yourself. Has your life come to a standstill? Do you have another marathon to run? A few weeks later, you have to go to the doctor's office. Wow. It's the news you did not want to hear; you are having a baby. What will happen now? What is going to happen to college? What will happen to that dream you had of a house to build, people to help, places you wanted to see, ministry you wanted to get into? What will people say? Forget all of that. What will God say?

So far in this chapter, did you see yourself through these pages? Do you know anyone who has been through this before, or can you relate to any of this yourself? Write your thoughts down. FREE YOURSELF FROM IT ALL. If you have never spoken a word about anything that you have been through or the race you are about to run, take this opportunity to let God in. Don't tell your secrets to anyone but Him. Read 1 John 1:9 "If we confess our sins, He is faithful and just to forgive us of our sins and to cleanse us from all unrighteousness." Never give up; there is no such thing as an ending, just a new beginning. In chapter fourteen, set yourself free; get free from it all.

Thank you for allowing the presence of God to fill you up. You are about to be amazed about what the Lord is going to do in your life. Now wait and see the wonders of His work. Hold on; you are in for the ride of your life. What He is preparing you for is worth the wait. Say, "Lord, use me for your glory this day, every day, and please don't allow me to have wasted time. Please don't let my mind go wandering off into space." Say to yourself, "I am a beautiful child of God, and I can do anything but fail."

As you run this race that God has put before you, do you even know how to run a race set before you, or are you just running your old life of guilt and shame, defeat and disobedience? You trained for this marathon; you may have to run this race just a little faster. Keep running until you cross the finish line. You have done some very wrong things in this world, and you have done everything people have told you to do that sounded like it came from God. Every person who has come into your life, you have listened to. Have you ever thought about listening to your heavenly father first and seeing what He has to say? Well, have you? Just take a good look at yourself. Is this how the Lord wants you to look? Now, look again. Are you doing what the Lord wants you to do, or told you to do, or are you just doing your own thing and living the way someone else wants you to live? Stop living on someone else's dreams and someone else's life; get yourself one. So what you've been through some things; so what you got fired from that job. Maybe

4

God was trying to tell you to move on to bigger and better things. So what you don't make as much as you should. Stop talking about it; make it happen; do better, get some help. Find another job, start that business, or help someone. Start thinking outside the box, then get out of the box and live. God's got you. Yes, you've been down some bumpy roads and saw some things you shouldn't have seen, crossed some paths you should not have crossed. You've stayed with people, slept on floors, caught the bus, didn't have too much or anything to eat. Your clothes are old, there's not enough money in your pockets, you've been abuse too many times, people hurt you, and maybe you even had kids before you should have. Whatever the case may be, you are still here, aren't you? Take a look at yourself. Smile, stick out your chest, show those teeth. When life gets so hard you don't know what to do, drop down on your knees and start praying, and don't stop until you get an answer. That's called "faith"; get some.

Every day you are here is a gift from God to get it right and keep it tight, and the secret to having it is to realize all the things that have kept you from finishing your race. Jesus died for all the things you go through, and no matter what you think about yourself, God said you matter. Don't allow people, places or things to kill your joy, your peace or anything God-given. What you went through already happened. Life can sometimes be difficult, but are you willing to endure to the end? Say to yourself, "Who I was existed, and I need my past and all my mistakes to get me where I am now.

The Lord will take all my mistakes and turn them into wonders of joy, for His glory, not for anyone else's. Oh God, when I lose hope because my plans have come to nothing....,then help me to remember that your love is always greater than my disappointments, and your plans for my life are always better than my dreams and my plans."

I remember something my mother always told me: invest in yourself; invest in your body by eating the right things and maybe doing some exercise, then invest into your spiritual being, allowing God's presence to fill you with more of Him. Then, make sure you get enough rest and don't abuse what God has given you. You know how we can get when we want to eat those bonbons and those glazed donuts with the icing on them. Then there's the pop, cookies, and please don't forget the ice cream and cake. Oh boy, what a dream! Yet, you are to invest in your soul and spirit by getting the word of God deep down into your body. Sit with Him; get into your prayer closet. If you don't have one, make yourself one by just going into a nice, quiet room where you and God can meet and have a loving relationship. Please don't make it all spooky. God is waiting for you there. He has room for you and anyone willing to come to Him. Meditate on what God's word says about your situation. You have been praying about some things, and yes, you are looking for an answer, waiting to hear from Him about all you have talked with Him about.

Next, you have to enjoy your peace of mind with Him, press your way though and enjoy the good life.

We all need a prayer life. In Psalm 138:8 it says, "though I walk in the midst of trouble, thou wilt revive me: thou shall stretch forth thine hand against the wrath of mine enemies, and thy right hand shall save me."

"The Lord will perfect that which concerned me: thy mercy, O Lord, endured forever: forsake not the works of thine own hands."

Then, in James 5:16 it says, "confess your faults one to another, and pray one for another, that ye may be healed. The effectual fervent prayer of a righteous man avails much." Now don't you feel better, a little lighter, without so much heaviness on your heart or head? That's because you allowed God to enter in and take control of the situation.

Chapter 2 –
As Your World Turns

What just happened? Stop thinking about it and start praying about it. Say to yourself, "my world is about to turn, and in this event, my life will not allow problems to turn against me like some of the things I worry about now. I will allow God to step in and fix it. I won't try and fix it myself." You know how life is; we get caught up in life so badly that nothing else matters. You know I am right. Stop putting your hope into the hopeless, and start with the savior, Jesus Christ, the one and only true hope for everything that we do. Don't permit yourself to settle for less than God's best for your life, and don't settle for emotional pain either.

Now, you have one more thing to worry about. Instead of taking care of things on time, which is part of life, we do just what we want to do, and we think it's okay. We always get caught up with "I don't care" attitudes., but what happened to order in life and responsibility? Order gives you peace, and you need peace so you can hear from God. Plus, we serve a God of order. Your world is about to turn, but without order, you will be distracted with many cares of the world. We can't divide our attention between stuff and God because it will prevent us from concentrating on Him and the destiny He has for us. God holds your destiny. Remember that. Stuff will have you so worried that it will take you outside yourself. Turning you from "at peace" to "no peace at all." There must be order at all times. We already live in a chaotic world. Don't you dare sit around allowing the devil to talk to you. You'd better be careful about what you hear and who you hear it from, and also what you say out of your mouth. Did you hear God's voice that one night? Did you? I am not saying that life won't hurt and things won't happen. What I am saying is, we have an awesome Lord and Savior, Jesus Christ, who is with us daily. He loves you and cares for you and knows just what you need and how you need it. He wants you to live your life to the fullest, but you have to allow Him in and stay focused on the prize. You will have disorder until you change your way of thinking because disorder will bring emptiness and a lack of meaning to your life. Then, frustration will set in with a little taste of loneliness and a breakdown of your life. Have you allowed loneliness in? There's just one thing; you are not alone. Think about the person you just slept with and how they feel. Now, it's time for both of you to seek the master and allow His hand to guide you both into His will, not yours. Please don't get distracted from this, or you will miss the blessings that the Lord has for you. This situation isn't permanent. You are coming out of this. Be patient. God is getting ready to turn your pain into a promise. Just wait on the Lord. Some of us are too impatient, but in Jeremiah 29; 11 it says, "For I know the plans that I have for you, declares the Lord 'plans for welfare and not for calamity, to give you a future and a hope." The Lord will always have your future in His hands; He is just waiting for you to let go. Don't allow your every-day routine to interfere with your walk with Him. So you messed up; so you had a child out of wedlock. Things will never be the same, so now it's time to be obedient to God. Be fair to yourself and want more than just what you have. Put God in charge of your life and wait and see what will happen. Please, allow me to share a little of my life to help someone out there. I thought that I was connected all the way with God all the time because things were going sort of good. But I started feeling lonely, feeling lost, and even worse, I felt forgotten by friends and family, and most of all by own children. But worst of all, I felt forgotten by God. I don't know if you've ever felt like this in your life, but it's real. Let me tell you about it so I can help someone out there. Let me start with loneliness first.

LONELINESS

This is a mind-blower. Not being connected made me feel alone. I thought about being single, with no man in my life, not being married yet, with my kids grown and no one in the house except me. Wow!!! That's real stuff, people. God talks about loneliness in His word. Revelations 3:20 says, "Behold, I stand at the door and knock; if anyone hears my voice and opens the door, I will come in to him and will dine with him, and he with me." This will take care of the loneliness; putting God in your life and enjoying His love and talking to Him about everything you need shows a personal relationship with Him. Then, in 1st Peter 5:7 it says, "Casting all your cares upon him: for he cares for you." God cares for you even in your loneliness; He wanted us to know that and to embrace it. God let me know that the life He has for me is much better than the one I have for myself. Now, allow me to go down the street a little bit with the act of feeling lonely.

FEELING LONELY

This will consume you every time and every day if you allow it to. I wanted to get to the level in my walk with the Lord where I could put my prayer life into action. I allowed the Lord in my loneliness and He consumed it, He covered it, He even fixed it. Are you hearing me, people out there? I had to do it or it would still be broken. Loneliness would still be hanging around and the devil would have won. Not in my life. To win, you have to allow the Lord in so He can fight the good fight for you.

Let's keep going on down the street some more until we run into "lost." Have you ever been down that street before, the street of "lost," where you can't find anyone or anything? I certainly have, and the road was bumpy. That road had so many deep holes in it I thought I was going to sink down to hell. That's how deep my thoughts were; that's how much I felt liking dying. You would not believe how feeling lost will make you feel. Stuff happens when things go wrong in your life and you don't know what to do about them and haven't let God in. Phil. 4:3 says, "I can do all things through Christ who strengthens me." Hang on to this because in your time of need, you are going to need it. Did you know that feeling lost will make you feel very empty inside? Stop and love yourself because if you don't love yourself, you won't love anybody else, and you won't be able to love God. God wants you to hear His words and believe them. He has a better plan for you, so when that old devil tries to stick his head out and you see him coming down your street, put the stop on him and hit his butt with the word of the Lord. Close your doors, shut the windows, and yes, that means you will have to read more. Stay on your knees; go into your prayer closet to have that personal relationship with the Lord. Life is life, and you can't stop things from happening. You just have to keep covered and get the whole Armour of God, which is described in Ephesians 6:11:

Put on the whole armor of God, that ye may be able to stand against the wiles of the devil. For we wrestle not against flesh and blood, but against principalities, against powers, against the rulers of the darkness of this world, against spiritual wickedness in high places. Wherefore take unto you the whole amour of God that ye may be able to withstand in the evil day, and having done all, to stand. Stand therefore, having your loins girt about with truth, and having on the breastplate of righteousness; and your feet shod with the preparation of the gospel of peace. Taking the shield of faith, where with you shall be able to quench all the fiery darts of the wicked.

And take the helmet of salvation, and the sword of the Spirit, which is the word of God:

God has all the answers you will ever need. He said in John 6:35, "I am the bread of life; he who comes to me will not hunger, and he who believes in me will never thirst."

Keep going down the street. There are more things; there's the feeling of "forgotten" on the crave side.

FORGOTTEN

This meaning is also powerful: unable to recall, overlook, neglect, sad, down, afraid, and even carelessness. I know what you are thinking. WOW! Just thinking about it is too much. Let me ask you this: have you ever pushed your prayers to the back of your mind? Have you ever felt like God has forgotten about you and your problems? When I was being abused (yes abused can I get free?), I remember it so well, even though the Lord has washed all the hurt and pain away. He has allowed me to help someone who may be going through this. I thought this was an everyday thing to where I thought it was the norm. I was crying out for help to my friends and family, crying out to the Lord for help, and I never got help. Tears used to run down my face so hard my eyes would close and turn red and swollen to the point where I couldn't see. All I knew was to cry out for help, begging the Lord to save me. "Where are you, Lord?" I cried out. "Do you hear me? This hurts," I said. "I need you right now. I won't make it if you don't come." The pain from abuse is a long road of healing. I used to feel like God had forgotten me for the choices that I have made in my life, and it was bad enough that people didn't care as well. We make our own choices, and sometimes make really bad decisions, but I truly thought that the Lord had forgotten about me and my problems. I was so sad and afraid, but I knew if I wanted to live, I had to let go of my past and the things in it and stop blaming myself and others for things I had done or allowed to happen to me. I had to speak life to myself and not death. What it boils down to is this: we are not to feel lonely, sad, forgotten, or even lost. These things are not in our make-up. The Lord did not make us up to be anyone's punching bag. That's all the devil's plan, but we are human and we allow things to take us there — problems like the children, singleness, not having kids yet, not having a husband, working too hard, or not having a job, or even having kids too early in life or the wrong way. Does any of this sound like your life? Can you see yourself through these pages? Well, I am going to tell you this: there is a God who loves big, and I mean BIG. He never forgets His loved ones. God will never forget about you; we will forget Him before He will forget us. We are children of God, created by Him, and nothing can separate us from that — unless you don't need him in your life. So, what's up with that? Do you? I feel that sometimes we want more than we are willing to give. We say God has forgotten us, but what have we done to remember Him? We only think about the Lord when stuff is happening in our lives, when all hell is about to break out, and we can't find our way around. Please don't get this twisted. We need God in everything and everywhere we go and do, but we need to stop playing with His feelings. Yes, God has feelings as well. He loves us so much that He gave His son Jesus. Do you think He had to do that for you? NO!!! We need to stop playing and start praying, stop taking God's love for granted. He loves us true enough, so let's start loving Him back, no strings attach. We have to know when God needs our everything.   REMEMBER THAT THERE'S ALWAYS A HELPER IN YOUR TIME OF NEED; HE IS JUST WAITING TO HEAR FROM YOU, AND HIS NAME IS JESUS. LET JESUS BE YOUR TURNING POINT, TO TURN YOUR WORLD AROUND, BECAUSE THIS IS "AS YOUR WORLD TURNS."

Chapter 3 –
When It Rains, It Pours

In this chapter, I will be talking about abuse and violence in the home. This subject is dear to my heart. In the last chapter, I touched on abuse just a little, but in the next few chapters, I will take it to another level and set someone free. I will give you some insights on it. I will even give insights about the children in the home, so sit back, sit up straight and take a deep breath. Here we go.

I would like to begin by saying I had a wonderful mother. She has gone to heaven now, but she raised me on her own, with the help of the Lord, of course. She instilled goodness and Godly ways into me at an early age. I am the oldest girl and the first to learn how to cook, clean and wash, sew and do it all. I went to church and had Sunday dinner together with the rest of my family. My mom raised me up the best way she knew how to. I have two brothers and two sisters, and I was the oldest girl. One of my brothers went to prison for a long time, and I never got to see him when I was young. I think he spent his whole young life in there, I'm not sure. He was a hard-headed boy and a "never listenes to his parents" kind of kid; you know how some of us can be when we are kids. I loved my brother no matter what he had done because our mother had instilled "love your family" in us, so it was easy to love others. Even so, when my brother did the deeds he did, I always told him that he could do better if he would try and listen to his heart. We all know right from wrong. God put that inside of us when we were little. It's our parents' part to instill it in us and show us the way. Don't get me wrong, we all have done some things in our lives, and we may or may not have good parents, or some may not even have parents at all, but some of us just don't talk about it. We just sweep it under the rug and try to forget it as life goes on. Please allow me to give you a life of pain lesson and just maybe you can learn something from what I am about to share with you. I am all about helping the helpless. That's why God has put me here to help His people in need. You see, we all need help but we just don't know how to ask. It took me a lifetime to even get to this level of asking for help, and sometimes I still don't say anything about it.

HOUSE OF PAIN

I am here to share my life of pain with someone out there who will listen. We all won't receive this and it may not be for everyone, but sit back, hold on to something and take a deep breath because the devil has just arrived on the scene riding on his horse; that was back then. For me, it started with abuse. I had never heard of the word before until I experienced it one on one. I know that it may sound very strange to say, but that's how it is. There's no two ways about it. Abuse is just what it is, wrong on all levels of the word. Don't let anyone say otherwise.

Now, with that out of the way, let me share my story. I was going to say "let me get free," but God already freed me from this years ago. You see, I thought that I was in love and he thought that he could control me in more ways than one. I was young and still wet behind the ears, had just turned twelve years old and wanted to taste life fast. I met this boy and fell in love with him from top to bottom. I didn't care what anyone said, I had to have him in all the ways that I could. I was twelve. What did I know about anything? But he did, so he had to work on me in other ways. He had to get my mind fixed to do whatever he said to do. We dated for years without me seeing this boy; we just talked on the phone and saw each other in school, at the dances in school — you know, everywhere young kids hang out. We never did anything until he had my mind. You see, when you are young, the devil is just around the corner waiting for you to do something wrong.

Without the Lord in our lives we are nothing, even at a young age. I knew right from wrong, had a good life; love was in the home and so was whipping. My mother was a single mom raising five children alone, working, cooking, cleaning, and loving on us, helping us with our homework, making sure we made it through school; she was helping us to be who God had called us to be, even when we didn't know what that was at the time. She was making sure life didn't get us too fast. I was in church; my mom made sure of that. I had my own room and dolls to play with, an Easy-Bake Oven, coloring books, just the girly things we as little girls needed to have. We weren't rich or well off. I come from the projects, but one thing was missing in my home, a FATHER. That makes all the difference in life. You can sit there and say "no it doesn't," but you would be lying to yourself and to others. The father's presence in the home sets the whole tone for the house. Yes, I had a talk-on-the-phone father, but he still came over and tore some butts up when things weren't right or when my mother would call him. He still stayed in our lives until he got remarried, then things changed with us.

DADDY'S LITTLE GIRL

I was daddy's little girl and the apple of his eye, but he was not in the home with me. At that time, I needed a word from my daddy. I needed him to speak into my life, to tell me about boys and the do's and don'ts. You know, sometimes we as women need the touch of our daddies. We need them to show us how a man treats a lady. If we can't see it in the home, show us any way; I needed that. I had other sisters, but I was the oldest girl and the one who worked the hardest for my parents to make sure everything would be good within the home. I even left school so I could help my mother out with the other kids and the house.

So now, back to my boyfriend from hell. I say this because he was on an assignment from the devil and he didn't even know it. I was turning fourteen now, and his assignment was me. I wasn't even aware of it; I just wanted to be free, being grown too early. My mom already had one child get pregnant at an early age and they always thought it would be me, but I was still beating up boys for touching on me. Well, this boy stayed in my ear night and day, day and night. You see, when the devil has his eyes on you, he will use whatever and whomever to do his will. This boy talked about me and himself like we were married, saying what I should and shouldn't do, how to act, how to talk, how to walk, and how not to talk unless he said so. Yes, this was a mind control thing and more. I didn't know this at the time; all I wanted was him.

I had just turned seventeen, and this is how it all started. Everything was good at first, I thought. I was good to him and he was good to me. I gave something God gave to me for my husband, but I gave it to a boy no older than I was. He told me that he loved me and that I was the only one he would ever love. He said to me that life was too short and I needed to live and get what it was I wanted; he said, "If you love someone, you are to share yourself," so I did. This was the lie of the enemy telling me just what I wanted to hear. That's how it starts, so guard what you hear and watch what you say.

Now came the loving he thought I would enjoy, the physical abuse. Let me define this a little as the use of physical force, force that may result in bodily injury or physical pain; that's love, you think.

Is this the need for love or acceptance much too far or much too great for anyone to fill? Did you know that it is often a void, or a need, rooted in abandonment at childhood; this will happen, but only to be filled by the love of an earthly father or resolved by the supernatural ministry of the Holy Spirit through lovingly administered deliverance. Never forget this one thing: words can hurt, and hitting isn't love. Don't get it twisted; even when we are so-called grown people, abuse is abuse.

Let's talk about some things that we all need to understand and believe: soul-ties.

UNHEALTHY SOUL-TIES

Mind, will, emotion, and desires; let me break them down for you a little. Your soul is the real you. A soul-tie is when something is cleaving together with you. A soul-tie is a means of one flesh, mind and one soul with another soul. At the core of it all, sometimes we are ignorant and not educated or free to see that we have allowed people to come into our lives and attach themselves to us. When we have unprotected sex without marriage, their mess becomes our mess, their crazy stuff becomes ours. Whatever nasty things they have done or said, thought, felt, or even touched in their lives is in us. In Hosea 4:6 it says; "my people are destroyed for lack of knowledge." What do you fear? You have to become free, and freedom is when you start to forgive others. If you are going to cleave to someone, let it be Jesus Christ. Loving Jesus more means you will avoid loving man too much and being attached to him, or even a woman, and this goes for everyone. John 8:36 says this: "if the Son therefore shall make you free, ye shall be free indeed."

Our minds – Psalms 139:14 "I will praise thee; for I am fearfully and wonderfully made: marvelous are thy works; and that my soul knows right well.

Our will - Luke 22:42 "Saying, Father, if thou be willing, remove this cup from me: nevertheless not my will, but yours, be done."

Our emotion - Matthew 26:38 "He that hath no rule over his own spirit is like a city that is broken down, and without walls.

Please take this to heart because this is someone's life out there. Things like this really happen. This is the real world, but people just don't talk about this. They sweep things like this under the old, dirty rug and act like it never happened. This is not the will of God for our lives, so take off those blindfolds, take the ear plugs out of your ears and hear, and see the word of God speaking to you clearly.

Do you want your life to have an impact? Focus on forgetting the past and look forward to what lies ahead. You can do this; you as a Christian in the body of Christ can do all things through Him. Don't leave anyone behind; take them with you. You are not in this world alone. Fix it.

This brings me back to something else happening in my life, me thinking I knew it all. We never know it all but think we have it together or can control something. Things have consequences, believe me, and look what happens. Read on.

Chapter 4 –
The Rise & Fall

The state of thinking you have it all together, forgetting what's ahead of you at the cost of who you are as a person and a child of God. Did you care about that when you found the love of your life, so you thought? No, it was a set up from the pit of hell, and you thought it was from the Lord Himself to you, His child. You had prayed and prayed for this to happen and asked the Lord to send a good person to you with a good heart and a strong mind, one who loves the Lord with all that's in him. But what did you get? Was it worth the wait, or did you even wait for them to come from the Lord? I know you were in a hurry to find them and begin your life. Yes, you got it. "Thank you, Jesus, for that person," you said. "Thank you, Jesus, for a new beginning." You started planning your wedding and looking for wedding rings, a house — you know, the whole nine yards. But one thing was missing. In all the excitement, you forgot to really check out the person you were about to spend the rest of your life with. Please allow me to start over from the beginning of this exciting story so someone can get blessed and free at the same time.

You are on top of the world with a great job, your own home, nice clothes, a car; you know, the things we need and want to make our life a little more complete, or just a little better, we think. But all that was missing was the one person we just couldn't seem to find to fit into our life, so we got the next best thing, thinking ,"that's for us." The trick of the enemy just came your way, and you got caught up. You were just minding your own business, working, going to church, reading your word and just trying to lose a little weight to make yourself feel better so when you did run into Mr. Right you would look your best. All that praying you were doing, God heard, but you just did not listen or see the signs from the devil. He was waiting for you in the wind of your mind. The enemy heard your prayers and put you in a trick bag. You thought you had Mr. Right, but instead you, the beauty, got the beast.

This happens when we look away from God and put your eyes somewhere else. Maybe you have heard about someone near or dear to you who has fallen. They have fallen so far down it seems like the pit of hell is right where they are. It seems the hole is so deep that they can't hold on any longer. They cry out, "HELP! HELP!" But no one hears their cry for help. Does this sound all too real for some of you, and real for some of your loved ones as well? Real talk. Are you desperately clinging on for dear life hoping not to fall all the way in? The trap has been made and down you go, lower than you ever been, so far you can't see the light above your head. You have just let someone into your life that shouldn't been there in the first place. You knew they were the one for you, the missing link to your chain. The warning signs were there, but you paid no attention to them. Time is passing you by, and you are not getting any younger. You waited on the Lord long enough, so you knew this was from Him; this is it. They dated you, so you thought. They took you to some places, and you thought that was great. They even wined and dined you at some point. But you said to yourself, "is this the best they could do for me? Is this all I get?" You said, "At least we are going somewhere and doing some things. Walks in the parks, going for car rides around the block or even to the store was fine with you; at least you had someone to call yours. Yes, but at what cost to you and your heart and your mind? Can you put a price on love and happiness?

As time goes on, you are getting deeper in with that person, so deep now that you are cooking, cleaning, and washing their clothes. My question is, did you have a talk on the way down the hole they were digging for you? Did you get any type of conversation with them, like what's the color of their eyes, or their hair? What are their habits, you know, likes and dislikes? What about their past or what's new for their future? Did you get any of that from them? Or were you so caught up with that person that you missed what you were supposed to be doing, which was interviewing them for the job of dating you? Have you missed the mark? Or have you allowed them to pull you in too deep, too fast?

When you are out there calling yourself dating and having fun, be careful what you set your eyes on and what you put your hands on as well. I guess the things we bring into our lives we never give a second thought sometimes. Doesn't this reflect on who you are as a person and your upbringing in life? All of it has a lot to do with the choices we make in our relationships as well. I feel it's called rushing, and why would you want to rush into a going nowhere relationship—a "may I take your order, have it your way" relationship? Stop settling for the do-gooders because the hole they are digging for you is not just a hole; it's a pit, an emotional, life-changing storm, a hole in the ground with nothing but misery and pain. Yes, you met someone you thought was the apple of your eye; you thought you struck it rich gold from Texas, the richest kind. But what it all boiled down to was they were setting you up for a fall, for a big disaster. That's what the wrong relationship could do for you.

Since you have this person in your life, they begin to speak into your life now. You already fell in the hole; their job is to push you in all the way. Have you had the bittersweet talk with your dream boat yet? They will have it without you even knowing. That's how slick the devil is; he has sent someone into your life as the good person you prayed to God for day and night. How can you go wrong with that? Has the whispering sweet nothings in your ear began yet, or the peck on your forehead because you said that you can do anything deep? Have they said that they can't live without you and that they need you to be with them all the time?

Those kinds of words will get you caught up in something you are not even ready for. Haven't you noticed a pattern here yet? They are fattening you up for the kill. They are about to talk about marriage and moving in together. You'd better watch yourself out there; it's coming. Have they used this one on you: "It's you and me against the world." You just fell in a little deeper. Deeper and deeper you go, and you haven't even realized it because it was so smooth. You see, the next move will be all yours. They won't have anything to do with it.

The very next time you saw each other, you talked about moving in. I bet you didn't see that coming, did you? You think that you are in control and you have them right where you want them. Think again, "baby." It's the other way around. They have you trapped in the goodie bag with no way out. Hey, have you ever stopped and thought to yourself, "How did this come about?" Well, let's review some of the pit falls. First, you set yourself up for a fall by allowing someone in your world you new nothing about. Then, you let them in without God in it. Did you hear from Him? Last and not least, did you turn to the bible for any of your answers or issues you were having, or did you think you were not having any? Were you that overwhelmed by what you were doing that you lost your focus and your mind? For one thing, the devil is real, and when you lose focus with God, things happen. Hey, I am not here to beat you up or even scare you to death. "Wait", I am just a little. You see, I can truly relate to this. I forgot to keep it close in my word and with the Lord as well. I know the pain all so well, but the more you read the more you will get to know His heart and how passionate He is. You will get to know His will for your life and what He has planned for you. I had to stop looking at the bible like it was just words that didn't make any sense. I had to ask for understanding first. I had to just do it, just pick it up and walk in it all the way. I wanted to feel and understand my Lord's heart, but that only comes from going on the trip with Him. Every time you pick it up and begin to read it, His love for you leaps off the page into your heart, the light in your soul comes on, and your life changes forever. The bible was written for you, and it's your personal guide to knowing and following God.

Some people may think it's okay to move in with the one they're dating but are not married to. Think about it. What would Jesus say about that? Don't settle for anything unhealthy because you will be missing the amazing time with God. He will offer you true intimacy. No more excuses that you are comfortable or you are a portrayer of needy and insecure. Is this what Christ truly desires for you to be in? This could be very poisonous for you. Or are you saying to yourself that you don't deserve better? In God's word, it says you do. Do you expect them to respect you, care for you, love you and not hurt you? But what have you done to get this? You show yourself as a weak person with very low thought for yourself. What I am asking is: are you a very needy person and do you try and make the other person happy and not yourself? Does this cost you your own happiness? Does that person cherish you or just consume your every thought? I know your mind has to be very tired, and it's full of different thoughts about a lot of things. You have experienced a mental meltdown followed by hurt and pain. The words of your parents and grandparents are ringing in your ear loudly. They have spoken the truth about what you should and should not do. But did you listen? No, you have fallen head-over-heels for that person because you want to feel like you belong to something beside yourself and your job and family. Right or wrong, you will take it. It's so amazing how we put the Lord into our mess and think it's okay. After all this talk, you still moved in with this person and began your new life, so you thought.

In the hole you go, a little at a time down, down, down. This time you went in more than the other times because this time you have gone off the deep end. It's moving day, and you feel like things are going so smooth that it's like butter, until they tell you that you can't bring all those things there. They did not even call it "things," they called it "junk." So you act like they didn't say a word and keep moving in. They stop you again and say, "I don't have enough room for all of your things. You will have to sell some of them." You see, this is how people do you when they are planning for your pitfall. WOW! Down the hole you go some more. You are so far down looking up isn't an option to you. You're just going with the flow. "Things will get better," you are saying. Have you stopped and asked yourself what happened, how did things get like this and why? What went wrong so fast? The trick of the enemy is always quick. Yes, you just made a foolish move. In the blink of an eye, you have fallen for utter foolishness and mayhem with some chaos to go. We always think that we know best, don't we? This is no one's fault but yours. When crazy things come your way, stop and check with the Lord on it because nine times out of ten, you had something to do with it, didn't you?

Now, allow me to bring the word into this; I want to do my own thing with whomever I want to do it with. Not on my watch. Let me put some word on it. In John 13:34, it says to love one another as Christ has loved you. When you really are in love, you want the best for each other in all things because true love isn't a selfish act; true love is willing to go the extra mile and wait, and wait patiently. This will allow the relationship to grow, all in God's timing, not yours. Are you respecting each other or are they only respecting themselves? They are to respect your thoughts and boundaries, not just tell you what to do, like it or not. Where is the respect in that? Have they ever given you emotional respect, or even encouraged you in some of the things you have going on in your life? Have they? What about encouragement in your spiritual growth? I tell you, people out there, choose wisely and be aware of what you are doing and saying. Choose your words and pray about everything. Allow me to speak on this. What about communication? Do you have any in all this mess, or are you so far down the pit that it doesn't matter to you? Well people, without communication you have nothing because that's the key to a healthy anything. Understand this as well: a person can only change if they want to, and you can't force them to or alter their behavior if they don't believe they're wrong. You see, they have been too busy getting you to see that wrong is good, and you haven't even noticed or read between the lines.

I know this feeling all too well because I've been there, done that. I used to be a wrong thinker, thinking the things that I was doing were the right things for me at the time, and putting more excuses with it. You know how we justify the means when it sounds good. Well, in God's eyes it was wrong, no two ways about it. We will let someone sweet talk the pants off us and send us in the deepest, darkest hole there is. Those kinds of people are smooth talkers and have slick tongues in their mouths. You know the ones the Lord asks us to stay away from. Well, your deed is done, and right now there is no coming back for you. You look up and can not see the sky anymore or even smell the flowers. You put your hand out in front of you and you are in utter darkness. You can't find your way out or touch anyone. You ask yourself what happened. How did you get there, and how did you get so deep in the pit? You ask yourself, "Can I recover from this? I love them so much and can't live without them. I have gotten older, and time waits for no one. I am strong, I can do this, and they are not as saved as I am. I will just have to out slick them and make them fall as well. I won't be in this hole alone, that's for sure." Two wrongs don't make a right, now, do they?

Chapter 5 –
The Secret of Abuse

L et me start off by talking about something that's dear to my heart, as I have mention before, abuse. I will try and give you some more insight on it. Let me start with Physical Abuse. This may include but is not limited to such acts of violence as striking (with or without an object), hitting, beating, pushing, shoving, shaking, slapping, kicking, pinching, and burning. Throwing something such as a phone, book, shoe or plate. Sometimes, it might be pulling of the hair, pushing, pulling, grabbing your clothing, or even using a gun, knife, box cutter, bat, mace or other weapon. This may even include smacking your bottom, forcing you to have sex or perform a sexual act with them, grabbing on your face to make you look at them or even just plain grabbing you period, because love is respect. Please realize that this behavior is wrong, and please don't make any excuses for the abusive behavior. Remember that it is never your fault.

Verbal and Emotional Abuse - This was a secret for years, not really understanding what was happening or why they felt so rotten inside. Or did they realize how easily mild forms of abuse can be the precursor to physical violence? Name calling again is an overt, obvious form of verbal abuse designed to hurt or degrade you. Terms of endearment can also be used in an abusive ways, when spoken with obvious sarcasm, for example. Threats are an overt form of verbal abuse, like yelling and shouting. Threats are designed to frighten us and verbally beat us into submission. Usually, we will be threatened either with pain or with loss, and the abuser will often choose threats based on his/her knowledge of what we value most or what we are most afraid of. Physical abuse threats can be as debilitating as the violence itself, but threats are also often made to prevent us from leaving an abusive relationship or to persuade us back after leaving.

Judging and criticizing are ways in which our partner shows his/her lack of acceptance of us as an individual. Phrases such as, "you always think you are right," are an example of judging; our abuser believes he/she can know and judge us better than we can ourselves. Comments disguised as being "constructive criticism" are often actually judgmental, critical and abusive. Statements starting with, "The problem with you" as blaming and accusing are self-evident, and retorts which are designed to shift the blame and the emphasis from abuser onto victim. While it is easy to pick up blaming and accusing, for instance, being accused of sleeping with someone else, it is not so easy to recognize phrases such as, "You always have to have the last word" as an accusation.

What's going through your mind as you are reading this? I think some of you are reading this saying, "if that was me." Is it you? Do you fit any of these statements, or have you ever been through anything pertaining to this? Do you know anyone who is going through anything like this? You might know someone. How would you help them, or are you one of those people who just looks the other way and doesn't get involved, saying to yourself, "it's not my business. They probably ask for it"? So, you think people in this situation asked for it, begged for it, or even said too much just to get it? Well, you are sadly mistaken. These people are human as well. Who gave you the right to judge others for what has happened in their lives? Did you get up and take a good look into the mirror? None of us are perfect; or did you forget that?

Sorry about that; I lost it for a minute, but I am back now. I have a story to finish.

FINISHED STORY

As time went on, everything was put in play; he had all the basics down; he just had to put it all together, test it out, and he did. It started with going to the movies with his sister and her boyfriend and other close friends of ours. We all were having a good time laughing, talking enjoying the movie; we even talked about how I was a square because I didn't get high or drink. I was a very nice person, pleasant to be around. On the way from the movies, during the bus ride home, he just kept saying, "when you get your 'blank' self to the house you better cook me something to eat."

I said that I needed to go home. "It's late. My mother wants me to come straight home after the movies."

This man said to me, "You should be afraid of me and not your mother," so I just kept on talking to everyone and didn't pay him anymore mind. When we got off the bus, he slapped me so hard that I fell down to the ground, and everything went black. My face was so red; his hand print was left on the side of my face. I wonder was I becoming his possession, his property. I ask this of myself. Everyone came over and picked me up and told him he was crazy for doing that.

This was just the beginning of it all. Yes, he said that he was sorry and he was not going to do it again, and yes I forgave him, and we went on with our lives. No, I never told anyone what had happened, and I had gone back to his house again because he was not allowed over to mine. My mother did not like him and that should have been some kind of sign for me, but it wasn't. I still went over his house. As I starting to knock on the door, he was already standing there waiting for me. He said, "come in," with a nasty tone. Right then and there I knew something was wrong. I went in and the hell began. I asked where was everyone, and he said "don't worry about it." I told him I should not be over there without his mother or older sister being there. But he told me to shut up and hit me with his fist. I fell to the floor and started to get very mad, then he hit me again and again. This man beat me so bad his sister came in and had to hit him in the head with a bottle to get him to stop. My face was so bloody and swollen; she asked me what I had said to him. As I wiped the blood off my face, crying, I looked up at her and said, "I did nothing. Call my mother. She said that she would take me home; she took me home and just dropped me off at the door and left. My family was very upset about the whole thing; everybody was crying and did not know what to say. My dad came over and said if saw this guy again, he would put him in jail.

We kept on dating, and without the hitting. That was the very last time he ever hit me or talked to me the way that he had. We ended up getting married and had kids together. I know what you are thinking. WOW!!! After all of that? Why? We had children together, so I thought it would get better, but it didn't. My son saw me, and this is what he did for me — I remember this all so well; one of my little ones said to me, "Are you okay? Does that hurt? Not knowing it, he went into the bathroom and got a towel, ran water on it, came back to me with it and said, "Mommy, here, this will help. Granny put this on my leg when I fell down. I grabbed him and just held him in my arms and cried out loud. He was only four years old, a little big boy. He wanted the hurt to stop and the love to come back. I stood up, fixed myself up and went into the kitchen to fix my little boy whatever he wanted. With tears in my eyes, God took the pain away while I cooked and started talking to me about what had just happened to me. He said that He came to wipe the hurt away, to dry all my tears away and give me back my joy. My son was four, and he did not ask any questions about who did what, he was so busy helping his mother feel better. After everything was said and done, I held my son and asked him was he okay and if he needed to ask his mother any questions about my hurt. He said "mommy, you are a good smelling, beautiful mother, with great hugs, and you cook good too. "He said that to me, holding my face with his little hands. "Momma, I love you, and you always said Jesus loves you too," and he kissed my hurt away, thank you Jesus.

CHILDREN THAT ARE IN AN ABUSIVE HOME:
How does domestic violence affect children?

Children from abusive homes witness violent behavior, sometimes on an daily basis; and sometimes they learn that it's an acceptable method for dealing with anger, and that some kind of violence is often passed on from generation to generation. Well, the devil is a lie. You'd better cast that lie down and remove those generational curses off your family. You'd better start putting some word on it, and allow the presence of the Lord and His word in it.

Children prefer to live in peace with both parents present, in non-violence and comparative security, even if it means living with only one parent if push comes to shove. Children who grow up in a violent home don't understand why this is happing to their family and why it won't it stop. Please allow me to finish if I can; tears were about to fall.

THE WORSE SIDE

After that, the abuse got worse. It went from all the above to ropes, chains, burning, stabbing, even trying to sell me to someone for sex, or sometimes using the kids to get to me — whatever it took for him to get me to do something for him. This time, he was trying to sell me in a bar to the first man with the most money. He had spotted a man, and this man knew something wasn't right, but he went along with it. He never touched me; he started talking with me, asking me questions about what was going on, so I told him everything. He came out and hit him in the mouth and said, "You should be ashamed of yourself. You need to be six feet under," and walked out of the bar.

After that, we went home, and he asked me what went wrong. I said, "He saw us when we walked in, and he saw you pushing on me and talking nasty to me." Yes, I could go on, but why? I did not learn from my lesson the first time around. We seriously don't consider the consequences of the choices that we make. I just wanted him and I thought that I could change him and make things better. But it wasn't me; he was the one who should have asked for help. Let me ask you this; have you ever become so preoccupied by what you wanted that you forget to be who you are?

Or did THEY TOUCH YOUR LONELINESS WHEN YOU WERE LONELY, did THEY TOUCH YOUR HEAD, YOUR HEART AND YOU'RE SEXUALITY, did THEY TOUCH YOU IN ALL THOSE PLACES AND

MORE? Did THEY TOUCH YOU IN YOUR LOWEST OF LOWS; did THEY TOUCH YOU THROUGH EVEN YOUR PAIN, did THEY? You Can't Go Backwards.

Let's talk about this. What's back there that you have to keep going back or just thinking about the past time? Was it good times back there? Was there love, peace or even happiness that you can talk about? Tell me something that will make me say wow, that's it. You can't, it's all a big lie that old devil has put in your head to make you believe it's okay to get abused or hit, or just cursed out sometimes, or that it's okay to get talked down to and not say a word about it to any one. You have allowed it so much you get to the point you say it's the normal thing to do; you need that person in your life, so you put up with all the stuff and all the hateful things they bring to your table. Allow me to ask you this: have you just sat back and looked at that person and said to yourself, "what am I doing? Is this all the Lord has for me, is this the kind of life God wants me to live? I know He made beautiful and smart, so what's my problem." Well there's nothing wrong with you or me, we just made bad choices, just like others do. None of us are perfect because if we were, we wouldn't need the father, Jesus, Don't you think so? Plus, He said no one is perfect or righteous; you just didn't allow the presence of God in to work it out.

Allow me to share a little more with you how I felt after the fact. I used to just sit around and think. Did you hear what I said? Used to. God healed me from all that mess and has allowed me to share things

42

with others. Well, here it goes: I used to sit at my table in the kitchen and wonder, how did I get here, how did this all come about, and why did I allow it all to happen? Were there any signs I missed, or was it there already and I was so blinded by love and sex that I missed it all? As a lonely person and a caring person who just needed much love and someone to love, I missed all the warning signs; believe me, there's signs. I just wanted things so badly and so fast that I wasn't trying to wait on anything or the right thing, or even God. We try to do it by ourselves no matter the cost or what we have to go through to get it done. We say "no one is going to understand what I am doing." But here's my response to that: while we are trying to figure it out, God has already worked it out. So I say yes to this: come to your senses and allow the presence of the Lord in and just sit back in your recliner and relax. Check yourself before you start anything or see anyone. First, know who they are, what they want in life, and where they're headed to, but first and foremost, do they know Jesus? Stop looking at their face and the muscles on their arms and legs and what shape they have. Pay attention to their minds and what is coming out of their mouths. Look under every rock; turn them over — yes, even the big ones as well — then climb to the top of every hill and see what you can see. Ask questions and more questions about them, their family, their job, their bad habits, what they do for a living. Don't just ask questions, listen for the responses as well, and stop all that smiling in their faces and all that day-dreaming about how you look good together. You'd better be the F.B.I., the C.I.A. and start investigating some stuff.

Let's talk about the secret ingredient that you don't know you have yet which is Jesus Christ. He has given you something inside of you to fight your way back to where He needs you to be. You see, He had a plan for your life, but you had a set back, and now God is about to give you a set up. I know that it sounds like too much, and you may even think it's too hard; you may even be afraid. You must not allow fear to latch onto any of your situations, not your mind, or even your spirit. Fear is cruel, and it's like a destructives disease setting up in your body, waiting to manifest inside and grow. You have to understand one thing; we are made to worship God. He gave all of us the means to worship. He gave you a mind, a soul, a body, a heart and a spirit, and nothing else should mater; not people, places or things should keep you from worshiping Him and doing His will. Don't let the fact that you just went through something deep and mind-blowing keep you from access to God. He gave you this. Jesus died for all of that mess, no matter what it is. No matter what you've been through, it was only a setback for your opportunity to a divine set up. This is a critical decision for you because you have allowed someone to take you to the breaking point like never before.

You sit there thinking to yourself, what have I done? Have I allowed someone to get to me in a way like never before? This person always had something nice/nasty to say about everything. I sit back and wonder if they really cared about me and my well being. Half the time they acted like they didn't hear me talking to them. I am sitting hear about to cry, wondering if I made the biggest mistake of my life. This person doesn't realize my love is for keeps, and I don't play around with the heart. I wonder have they ever loved anyone before. Yes, it hurts a little, and I am sad about it. Maybe I should just leave, but where do I go? I am stuck. Have you ever found yourself in this way before making life-changing mistakes and decisions? What do you do when life don't seem fair, and you ask God, what did I do wrong? How did you deal with it when it wasn't expected? How do you manage your miracles when you and your miracles live with your misery? How do you survive an unbearable situation?

I am here to encourage you that you are going to make it through this storm as well. You are going to survive. Just don't quit; don't walk away; put God's word on it; pave the street with it; wash the walls with it; just don't quit because the Lord has something to say about this matter. Believe me, He does. Please don't allow the fear of leaving to cause you to ignore the pain to stay.

A right-now God is right in the middle of your situation. "A soft answer turns away wrath, but a harsh word stirs up anger.

The tongue of the wise commends knowledge, but the mouths of fools pour out folly.

The eyes of the Lord are in every place, keeping watch on the evil and the good.

A gentle tongue is a tree of life, but perverseness in it breaks the spirit" (Proverbs 15: 1-4).

YES YOU CAN!

If you don't change your situation, your situation will change everything about who you are and who God needs you to be. God never chose for you to be abused by your spouse or anyone else in life. He said you were to give up your life for the gospel's sake, not for someone's sickness. Don't allow yourself to be abused; it will say that you really don't love yourself enough to get away from it. Sometimes it may be easier said than done. If God loves you enough to let His precious Son die for you, then you are very valuable, so you must love yourself. When you stay, you are also abusing yourself and all that God created you to be, so call someone, do something. Sometimes, the only call you need to make is to call on Jesus. When life knocks you down, Jesus will pick you right back up. God is stronger than your weakness, and your story isn't over yet. You are not even finished yet just because things happened; you've done things you shouldn't have done; you even said some things you shouldn't have said. It's okay. It's not what people, family, friends, or even your children say that will break you, but it's what you choose to hold on to and believe that will eat away your hopes, your dreams, your joy and even your peace, until the faith you have is gone right out of you. So turn all of your misery to a miracle from God. The secret isn't to change for God, but to allow Him to change you. God doesn't want perfection, He wants obedience; remember that, and until God sees your heart, He will still love you the same. He is an amazing God that will come and rescue you when you need Him the most.

God is about to open new doors for you, so get ready with prayer so you can stay positive. Don't have a negative mindset. It will never get you the results you want in life. Staying strong makes people wonder how you're still smiling, and when God is your focus, you can do what people say you can't do. Don't let the now you sabotage the next you. Know who you are in Christ always.

WHO ARE YOU IN CHRIST?

Chapter 6 –
A Child's Secret (In the Home)

With all this talk about abuse, what about the children? What have they seen? Do you think they saw anything or heard anything, and how do the kids feel about it? I saw the faces of my own children when I was going through it. You try and keep your children from seeing you crying or even allowing them to see you with a swollen face, or bleeding. Someone out there had to hide the fact they had broken arms or legs. How do you hide that from your loved ones, and why should you even have to? Because someone you loved hurt you. At times, you didn't know what was going to happen with you; you were just trying to survive. Just in case you have never looked into the eyes of a child after he's seen you get beaten, let me try and tell you about it.

My children were little, but children still know when something isn't right. They can hear it in your voice and see it in your eyes. They can smell it on you as well; you just can't hide that. I had too many instances of putting on a fake smile with pain going through my body. I even had to help my children with their homework when there was fear in my eyes of what was going to happen next. Don't have older kids; they know what's going on, and they keep asking you why you allow their father, or that man or that person, to hit on you and talk to you like you're nothing. Older kids won't understand. Children are expected to keep secrets. Some kids put blame on themselves thinking they said or did a particular thing. Sometimes, they become angry with you as their mother for allowing the abuse to happen. Some children may be starving for attention, affection or even love. A woman is struggling to survive, and the abuser is too busy assuming control of everyone and every situation.

Let's talk about boys in the home who see their mothers abused. They are more likely to batter their partner as soon as they become adults, and girls may result to threats or even violence, thinking that's the norm in their relationship. Some children from violent homes may start to drink, do drugs or have stress disorder, or just run away from home to get away from it all. I can relate to that. My boys saw too much when they were young, but I tried to do all I could do to keep their little young eyes from seeing any incident of physical or sexual abuse. I didn't want their little ears to hear any threats or fighting noises coming from anywhere in my home. I tried so hard to keep their little eyes from even observing such things as blood, torn clothes or broken items in the home. My children didn't know anything until they got older and I told them about it, but sometimes it's easier said than done; I used to say, "Hurt me if you have to, but not my babies."

This is just some of the impact children have in an abusive home. Children impact a lot in the home. You try to keep them from getting hurt, and at the same time you try and stop the hurt. I know that you will not allow your babies to get hurt, and you will go through anything to protect them; I sure did. My children were not supposed to grow up seeing things like that, a man putting his hands on their mom or hearing pain coming from my voice. I used to cry out, "Lord, help me. Help me get out of here. I am your child. What did I do? Nothing." I cried out, letting God know who I was and how this hurt. God knew the things that I was going through; He knew the pain that I was having because He is an all-knowing God. I just didn't understand why He was allowing this to go on.

I know there are some questions you ask God yourself, and you may even dislike Him for not caring enough to get you out. You see, God had given me plenty of time to get away from it all. I just didn't see it. I was so consumed by my mess that I was not paying attention to the signs of escape. You see, sometimes we get so caught up with our stuff, our mess, what's happening to us that we miss the way out. Then God will send His people along in your life to push you out of it and into your destiny that He has for you. So people out there, stop sitting on your God-given bottoms acting like you don't know anyone going through something, anything. I truly feel that we are put here in this world to help others see the light of God. We are to help push love ones, friends, family, and all the unsaved; they want to be helped into God's loving hands. Don't sit there and act like you don't understand what I am saying. But this needs to be said. I don't want to end on a sad note, but the Lord will wrap this up for you and wrap His loving arms around you and give you and your children a great big hug, just to let you know that He loves you and He does care deeply about you and your children. He loved us first. God will restore all broken hearts, so don't allow your bitterness with people from your past to control your future, and never forget the price He paid to free you.

Before I move on, allow me to express how I used to pray each and every day for my children's safe keeping of their minds and hearts. I feel kids who grew up seeing too much and hearing too much will turn out to be the mirror image of their parents. My children did not see much, but they heard a lot of things they should not have heard. But I must say they have turned out to be the most respectful, caring, loving young men. I had the God-given strength to raise them up okay. Yes, I had to allow God to be in my life so they could see how and where I get the strength to carry on, the wisdom to get them through, the love to carry them when they got into trouble, and the patience for them as they got older. This is what the Lord will do for you if you let Him. Now I am ready to move on. The love of God is the key to getting free from anything. God love will continually grow and strengthen you when you walk in the light of His presence.

Allow me to talk about the recovery from all the things you have been through. Recovery means finding a new meaning to living, and keeping your fear of being hurt again. Don't you know talking about it is another way of recovery from the silent mold? You need to take action on your past or present life before you do anything else. Have an action plan. You are going to need it because your children witnessed domestic violence in their home, and might be holding a secret within them.

What behaviors do children who witness domestic violence exhibit? Do you even know? Do you even care? Well it's this:

The emotional responses of children who witness domestic violence may include fear, guilt, shame, sleep disturbances, sadness, depression, and anger (at both the abuser for the violence and at the mother for being unable to prevent the violence).

Physical responses may include stomachaches or headaches, bedwetting, and loss of ability to concentrate. Some children may also experience physical or sexual abuse or neglect of their own. Others may be injured while trying to intervene on behalf of their mother. What kid do you know who wouldn't try and protect one of their parents?

The behavioral responses of children who witness domestic violence may include acting out, withdrawal, or anxiousness to please. The children may exhibit signs of anxiety and have a short attention span which may result in poor school performance and attendance. They may experience developmental delays in speech, motor or cognitive skills. They may also use violence to express themselves, displaying increased aggression with peers or their mother. They can become self-injuring to themselves or maybe others. Children from violent homes have higher risks of alcohol/drug abuse, post traumatic stress disorder, and juvenile delinquency. Witnessing domestic violence is the single best predictor of juvenile delinquency and adult criminality. There is a definite correlation between domestic violence and child abuse.

Growing up in a violent home can set patterns for children ... patterns that can cause them to commit violent acts and more, or even continue the cycle of violence when they get married and have kids. Only Jesus can heal the wounds left by abuse. Sadly, many hurting people are waiting for the abuser to come repair the damage they caused. While it is good for the abuser to take responsibility and make amends to those he or she hurt, it is Jesus who grants peace to those in pain. He is neither unaware nor apathetic to those who suffer, especially children. That should give us pause, knowing we are accountable for the suffering we cause to others. The Lord Jesus cares for His people and has laid down His life to demonstrate His love for you. He will most assuredly comfort, vindicate, and heal you. The Bible regards abuse as sin because we are called to love one another, and abuse disregards others and is the opposite of this command. An abuser desires to satisfy his natural selfishness regardless of the consequences to himself or others. Everyone is guilty of abuse at some level because everyone falls short of God's command to love others sacrificially. Only the love of Jesus in us can truly love others; therefore, real love only exists in those who have accepted Jesus as their savior.

I felt that children who witness domestic violence see too much. SEEING: an incident of physical or sexual abuse. They also hear too much. HEARING: threats of fighting, noise from other parts of the house. Then they observe too much after the fact of the abuse; blood, tears, or even broken items. If you want something you've never had, you have to do something you've never done. What is it that you want? What do you want for your children? Choose faith over fear. You can overcome anything to protect the ones you love; give them to Jesus, and allow Him to work on you and them. You owe them that for the things they have seen and felt. Give your little ones something you've never had. Wrap your loving arms around them, and all of you guys breathe the breath of life together. One, two, three, here it comes; catch it all in. Now cry a little and move on. Life is too short to be stuck in one place.

Have you ever seen your life from God's view? What does this mean to you? The more you get from God, the more He wants you to be responsible. No, He expects you to be responsible, for your actions, for your way of thinking, for your way of doing things. Don't you know that you were created for much greater things? What will you live for? What will you stand for? Will you live for your own selfish gain, your family, your children, your husband, your friends, or maybe your own pleasure? In Romans 11:36 it says, "For of him, and through him, and to him, are all things: to be His glory forever Amen." Amen to that. Everything comes from

God, and everything we live for is by His power, and everything is for His glory and His glory only.

Don't ever get it twisted and think it is luck. NO, it's JESUS.

Chapter 7 –
All Grown Up
(School – Drugs & Prison Life)

I just knew one day I would have to share my story with others. If I could help someone out there to not go down the road I went down, why shouldn't I help? That's my God-given duty. I have four boys, and out of my four boys, three of them went to prison. I had three in there at one time, a mother's nightmare. It started first back in the middle of the 2000 decade, about 2006. My boys were grown and on their own with lives of their own. Two of them had children of their own and wives as well.

Allow me to share about the first son. He went down when he was young. He thought that he would be disobedient to his parents, stay out of school, steal, curse, cut school, the whole nine yards. Me, I was not having it. I was a strong woman but had problems of my own. I had problems, and I didn't want to go through any madness with a disobedient child. You know how it goes; house rules or else. Do right and what is expected of you. You see, he thought that his life was so hard and unfair and that I was making a difference with the other children. There are two younger siblings and they just needed a little more attention; one was an asthmatic and had other problems. The truth is he just wasn't aware God was setting him up for his destiny. He just wanted to be a hard ball who wanted to have his way. We have to go through something to get where God needs us to be, yes even as children. You're not different, just young and still have a chance to get it right and keep it right. Now, my oldest has a wonderful head on his shoulders and doing just great, praise God.

Then there's my second son who went to prison as well, for wanting too much too quickly. He was attending a very nice school where he went from a troubled child to an awesome young man with a great future waiting for him and he didn't even know it. God was in his life and had placed a gift in his lap. College was paid for and the whole nine yard. This son of mine left school with a 4.0 school average, enough to make a mother very proud, so as a mother we do the best we can for our children. I did not have money, worked from dusk to dawn and was taking care of two young boys, my mom and helping out the family. Tell me this: what have you done when the Lord has placed something great into your life? What did you do with it? I myself just started placing his things in order, you know, the things kids need for school, bed items, hot plate, all the things to survive. I did not have much, but God gave us all we needed to get by. First, I needed my children to take the Lord everywhere they went, even school, and also to make sure they put Him first. This son wanted more than just school. He was bored of that but was enjoying the life of college. He stayed, of course, because he knew I'd spent all I had on his future; I took everything out of both of my accounts and did what I had to do. You see, I had to do that for my children. My mother and his brothers helped as much as they could, and that's what family does for each other.

My son was living his dream of going to school and becoming someone in life. He always talked about growing up and helping his family, having houses built and helping with paying off things and just lived a God-fearing life. He was a good young man and always tried to help others always, and loved his brothers and his family a lot. My son spent half of his life taking care of my mother as she got old. He always went over her house to help with the shopping and the cleaning. They were thick as thieves. He called her Granny Gummies, which was her nickname from all of my children; they all took turns caring for my mother. She was so proud of him; she was on a fixed income and always wanted to help out with his school.

He even saw his dad for the first time in a long time. He helps out as well. Children need fathers to help push them. There's just something about fathers that God gives them power to push their kids in the right way through life. Now, life is about to hit him hard. My son's way of thinking made a turn for the worse. He had become disrespectful and just unbearable to live with. Yes, he had turned to selling drugs. I did not know for a long time because he did not want to disappoint me. He wanted the quick money. Some may think that this is the way to go for a little while just to make ends meet. Well, let me open your eyes on some things you may or may not know. There is no such thing as "fast money," of money that grows on trees or in back yard. For me, it gave me hell. I wasn't expecting it. My son went from selling drugs, staying out late, and staying up late, to prison. That's the life of a person who wants quick money. I had a long talk with him and said this to him: "If you didn't like what you were doing, you should have changed the game, not started selling drugs."

He didn't just go one time; he had to go another time because he didn't learn his lesson the first time. This time, he went from drugs to hanging around the wrong people and getting shot at; people even wanted to kill him. He went back to prison, and yes, I headed him down, kept money on his books and made sure that he had what he needed, not what he wanted. God had blessed me with a great job, so this time I had the money to do this for the both of them. My son had always said if he ever went to prison don't come there. It was hard not to. I was about to have three of my sons gone to prison. My first visit was a fearful one because when those doors close behind you, you are locked in as well. You can't wear this or that, you have to get check and you can only seat in front of them. No touching or kissing; it was like you were in prison as well. There used to be a lot to talk about in a short time. I hated it; one reason is because when it was time to go, my son always got so sad, and began to cry. Yes people, when your freedom is taken away from you, what can you do? Nothing but cry.

My son always told me that he was not going there to find God; he came in there with him, so Jesus would be there when he got there. You see, some people go to prison and find God not knowing He is everywhere you need Him to be. I have taught my children about Jesus and all His works. Now you sit back and see if they will apply it to their lives. My mother used to say that everyone must know Him for themselves. My son went with a good heart knowing just what he had to do to survive the storm. He did not know what to expect, but he just had to allow God to show him the way. He knew about the one road leading to hell; that road would break him up and he would fall and die. God had a plan for his life, and he wanted to find out what that was. I used to send them spiritual things, a bible, little notes with bible verses on them. They had to get it for themselves, and when they did, they were sharing it with others.

The last son to go down was my second to the oldest. He was not thinking about prison when he did something wrong. You see, someone had touched his daughter, and he found out and went to see her; then everything fell apart. He could not see straight. He could only see red, and did the only thing he saw fit to do, which Was shoot this person and ask questions later. This son of mine was gentle, kind, loving and would give you the shirt off his back. His daughter had to be between five and six years old at the time. He as well did drugs and drank and was just a nice/nasty person. You can't be both. One will come out more than the other one. God had to put him down so that He could pick him up. He had to do five years, and it was very hard on him, and most of all on all of us. I had to take his daughter down there with me. I did not want his daughter to be a prison kid where she would spend her young life going back and forth. She loved her daddy, and he loved her. This was his only child as well. This was his first time, but crime doesn't care about age or color or if you have a wife, a husband or children.

Now, I had to see two sons in the same place. My oldest was getting out. This was so hard for me, taking care of two children in the prison system, but as a strong, God-fearing mother, I had to do it. There are so many boys in prison now, and their parents or anyone don't do anything for them. On the list of frightening things a parent fights with, such as low education, low income, being a single parent and on top of all that the location of where you raise your children up at, is a significant factor. Plus the fears of having your son or daughter commit a crime and go to jail or prison has to be among the worst on this list. A parent who loves their child cannot help but feel some level of anger over what has happened. The first thing is to deal with the reality of the whole situation within oneself. It is normal to have some kind of feelings of denial, shock (you're shocked that's it your child), anger because you want to grab them and just pour the right thing into their heads, and grief because you will be missing them very much and might have to take care of their children. Now that's real talk. You might have to reach out for support from trusted friends or family. Please don't get those friends who, as soon as you get off the phone with them, put it on FaceBook. And as far as family members go, you'd better call on your granny, or your mother, but first, call on Jesus. Self-blame or blaming others, including one's child, will not help the circumstances. Know that in this day and age there is zero tolerance, and children who commit crimes are judged much more harshly than in the past. A parent needs to be courageous and know that people will likely assume things about them and their child that may not be true. They need to know that they did their best as a parent regardless of what others may think. Naturally, every parent makes mistakes, some more serious than others. However, the shame or guilt can be a barrier to continuing to be the best parent possible. Even in the worst criminal cases, a parent's continuing love and support can make a whole lot of difference. Stick by your child; he or she is your child, and if you won't who will? Don't throw them to the wolves like your butt didn't make any mistakes in your life time. It does not mean that you condone whatever crime occurred, it only means you are there for them.

Spiritual support can be essential to dealing with the situation as well, especially on a day-to-day basis. Jesus makes a world of difference in your life, and prayer changes things always. This has been one of the hardest things I had to do, besides laying my mom and dad to rest.

Now, let's talk about when they come home. Your initial goal when that happens should be to secure a place where you can stay after being released. Parole conditions will probably dictate that you cannot be homeless, and an important part of successfully transitioning from prison life into the "real world" again is to find housing. If you do not have a place of your own to go back to, make arrangements to stay with a family member or a friend until you can afford a place of your own. One major mistake made by many former inmates is that they fall back into associating with people who may lead them astray again. Ties can be hard to ignore, but do everything you can to place yourself in a situation that will enable you to avoid legal infractions, even if it means avoiding interactions with certain friends and family members. The guidelines of your parole will probably prevent you from living or even associating with ex-convicts, and it is important that you place yourself in a positive environment with people who are reliable and law-abiding. Also, avoid unhealthy relationships with people where there is potential for abuse or violence or who simply want to prevent you from being successful. Life after prison can be emotionally difficult due to the degree of sudden change and the fact that many former prisoners may still be haunted by past experiences. Taking advantage of counseling opportunities can give you the tools you need to deal with such feelings successfully and improve your mental health, which is of utmost importance in facing the challenges that lie ahead.

The United States has the largest prison population in the world, and the second-highest per-capita incarceration rate which in 2014 was around 735 out of a population of about 92,000. In 2013 in the US, there were 698 people incarcerated per 100,000 of the total prison population. This is the U.S. incarceration rate for adults or people tried as adults. Persons who violate state laws and/or territorial laws generally are placed in state or federal prison.

As of 2004, state prisons proportionately house more violent felons, so state prisons in general gained a more negative reputation compared to federal prisons.

"1 n 5 Black Males Will Go to Prison In Their Lifetime. One in every five black males born today can expect to go to prison." Did you hear that? "Expect to go" — who said that and why? Compare this with one in every six Latino males, and one in every 17 white males. Blacks are also far more likely than whites to be stopped by the police while driving. Blacks and Latinos are generally poorer than whites; they are more likely to rely on court-appointed public defenders, which tend to work for agencies that are underfunded and understaffed. Drug wars led different countries' populations of incarcerated drug offenders to soar higher than you could even image. Drugs are out there. You may or may not believe that; just look around and open your eyes. African Americans constituted about 13 percent or more of drug users, but they make up about 46 percent of those convicted for drug offenses. The numbers say that there are more black men in prison than there are in college. What are they saying? They'd better count them again. As time has gone on, the number of black men in college has risen. See what I am saying?

Well, all three of my boys are out and doing great. My

first one, which was my oldest, lives out of Cleveland, works at a great job and has one son of his own. My second son, which is my second to the oldest, is married with four children—three girls and a son of his own. He has a good job and is about to start his own business. Lastly, there's my third son, which is my third to the oldest. He has one son of his own and works a great job, and he just finished school for massage therapy. God had a plan for all their lives and had to put them down on their backs so they could look up to Him. Don't get it twisted; no one is perfect, and God said He would never leave you nor forsake you. I thank the grace and peace of God for bringing all three of my boys out and making them great, God-fearing men, so if anyone out there has sons, daughters or even family members in prison, please don't just leave them there for the things they have done. Ask God to forgive them for their sins and create in them a clean heart. He will do it. Who are we to judge people for what they do?

In the next chapter, I will talk about some of the reasons some people go the way that they do; maybe it's a broken heart. You know, when your heart is broken, your head doesn't work; I pray that this helps someone out there to move on and get peace from God.

THE BROKEN HEARTED

When your heart is broken, your dreams are destroyed, and your mind is so confused on what to do next. A broken heart can cause such an intense reaction that you may feel your life has been completely stripped of meaning. Jobs, hobbies, or friends may no longer hold any joy for you in your life. It's time to heal all wounds; it's something we have all heard over the years, but do you really have to wait for time to heal all your wounds? No, you do not. There are some small steps you can take to soothe the pain you feel. First, you should get with the problem solver, Jesus Christ. My sons had broken hearts and they just didn't know it. Allow me to explain. My first son had a broken heart; he went to jail at a young age and then went to prison on top of that. First, he got married young. She had a baby. They did not have much between the two of them, just each other and with a child that's not much. You see, if you are going to do the thing, make sure you are prepared first. My son had to move in with me, him and his family. He had to work at a job that did not pay much, and he had to do all the things for his family real grown ups had to live for.

How do you live right when your heart hurts so bad? One thing led to another, and she went away for awhile. My son just could not take it anymore. He could not take care of his son and live his life, so I had to get his son while he lived his life, or tried to. I had their son for about three and a half years, putting my own life on hold for a while. You se,e life is funny; it will take you for a loop if you let it. We want the good life and the fast life all wound up into one. Well, after a while of praying and fasting, things got back on track, she came home and he got himself together. But the very sad part of this was she took my grandson with her after I had him since he was almost one year old. When he left, he was four, and that was the last time that I saw him until his sixth birthday. Now, my grandson is about to be sixteen years old, and God has dept him and loved on him as well. He is very good in school and on his way to bigger and better things in life.

Now let me talk about my next son's broken heart, He got into so much trouble doing things he normally didn't do, going places he never would go and just had this "I am grown" attitude about life. Don't tell me anything. He knew it all. My son was smart and would help others, but his heart was broken and he just would not get help. My mother had passed away while he was gone away to college, and they were very close as I mentioned. She was Granny Gummies to him and his best friend. They would always go places together and talk about the bible a lot. Her friends knew they had a very special relationship, and love overflowed between the both of them. But now his heart was broken. He stopped going to school and came home from college. He was at Alabama State College doing great, but when he got the news he wanted to come home. After that, things went downhill for him. Trouble was around the corner waiting for him. The devil was sticking his head out, waiting for him to come down his street, and down he went. My son went to prison for four years, and he took his broken heart with him.

My other son, the last one, got his heart broken when someone touched his daughter and took pictures of her. Who in their right mind — yes, in their right mind does that to a little girl? I know that there are people out there with that mind set, but we need to love on our children more and keep them in a two-parent home, with the presence of the Lord all around them. Our children are sweet little love buckets for whom we have to do all it takes to allow them to grow. My son is much better now, and his little girl is not so little anymore. These stories let you know that if your heart is broken your mind doesn't work. I am not saying that this is in every case, but I do know in many cases, when things are not right, or the means are not there, children take the so-called easy way out for some of them.

Ephesians 6:
"Children, obey your parents in the Lord: for this is right.

Honor thy father and mother; which is the first commandment with promise;

That it may be well with thee, and thou may live long on the earth.

And, ye fathers provoke not your children to wrath: but bring them up in the nurture and admonition of the Lord."

Colossians 3:20
"Children, obey your parents in all things: for this is well pleasing unto the Lord."

John 3:16
"For God so loved the world that he gave his only begotten Son, that whosoever believeth in him should not perish, but have everlasting life."

The Bible has a great deal to say about the way we can successfully raise our children to be men and women of God. As a good parent, we must first teach the things true and good about God's Word. As a good parent, it is important to involve your child in church and with family and ministry when they are young. Regularly attend a Bible-believing church, (see Hebrews 10:25), allow them to see you studying the Word, and also study it with them. Discuss with them the world around them as they see it, and how they feel about the things they see. Also teach them about the glory of God through everyday life. "Train a child in the way he should go, and when he is old he will not turn from it." (Proverbs 22:6).

Being a good parent is all about raising children who will follow your example in obeying and worshipping the Lord first. Children who grow up in undisciplined households feel unwanted and unworthy. They lack direction and self-control, and as they get older, they rebel and have little or no respect for any kind of authority, including God's. "Discipline your son, for in that there is hope; do not be a willing party to his death" (Proverbs 18; 19). At the same time, discipline must be balanced with love, so our children won't grow up to be children who are resentful, discouraged, or even rebellious with their parents or other people.

Raising Your Children? Great Job! Tell God About It.

_____

_____

_____

_____

_____

_____

_____

_____

_____

_____

_____

_____

_____

_____

_____

_____

_____

_____

_____

_____

_____

Chapter 8 –
Your Assignment (What is it?)

What were you put here for? What do you think you are supposed to be doing? Are you supposed to be locating your assignment while you are here? I feel that we all were born for a certain assignment. So, the next time you run into life's troubles, instead of running the other way, ask yourself: what is your assignment, and how do you find it? Ask yourself what your milestone in life is; ask yourself what your mission is as well. Don't you ever think that taking care of children or your husband or your family, or even your job is all God has for you to do? You should be reflecting on your life; it may hold the secrets to your life's assignment. You have to truly understand yourself; this will help you to prepare for repentance. God designed you to thirst for him. He gave you choices so you could allow the thirst for Him to burn inside your hearts. So you would desire more and more for Him, and it will never stop, and the flames will never go out. Did you know that any actions or response that flows naturally from your life's circumstances comes with limited information? God may or may not give you all of the information, but He will release just enough information so you will keep obedience to His will, to His agenda, and always to Him. We were created to worship God and walk in our assignment. Has God ever given you an assignment to the point that you just knew what it was? What did you with it? Have you ever said to God, "Here I am. Use me on Lord, your will for my life." Have you realized that your assignment comes from the heart of God and also comes with eternal consequences? Wow, that's deep.

Let me share one of my assignments with you. One of my assignments was to take care of my boys and see them through, from school to prison and back home again. Life will take you for a turn sometimes if you allow it to; it has its ups and downs, but remember this always: God is there behind every door, in every closet and under every rock you turn over in Jesus' name. I had to see my boys through until the Lord said to me one day, "Enough, let them go on their own." I was doing too much for them when they got out of prison. I went overboard with my assignment from the Lord. I started taking things into my own hands and put more on myself than I could bear. This wasn't God's will for my assignment. I went off the deep end. You see, when the Lord gives you an assignment to do, do it right until He says enough. Don't carry it too far, more than He said to. We should stop putting more on ourselves than the Lord put on us. We need to get our assignments and work them, love on the Lord and keep it moving. Who are we to make things up and add on and take away? He said to be obedient and do His will.

One of my other assignments was to work at the airport for a certain number of years and leave when the Lord said to. Well, he did, and I stayed past His time for me. So, wrong things started happening in my life. I started sinning more, doing things I knew were wrong and did not care one bit about it. At my job, people started to lie on me for no reason, or one reason or another. It just did not make any sense whatsoever, the things that were going on in my life. I never thought about my assignment the Lord gave to me years ago. I was just moving on, doing my own thing and stopped caring about what God had said to me. Wow, was I in big trouble with my father. So, He left me in my mess for about three years after I was supposed to leave. I was only supposed to stay for four years, not seven. God left me in my mess that much longer until He got me out for good. He had to work on my heart, my smile, my love and my obedience as well. God had to make me humble. He broke me to no end, until I gave up and said, "Father, I will." I had to ask for forgiveness more than once; I had to fast, pray, get on my face and in my prayer closet. I had to stay in God's word night and day, and when my three years were up, His release was in the wind for me.

God already had my next assignment, and I was very ready to get to it. What has the Lord put in your spirit for you to do? Where did He say to go that you were not ready to go there? Think about it. We all have things in this life to do and people to see and places to go. God has given everyone an assignment! We each have a position in the Body of Christ and a distinct mission to fulfill, and God has perfectly equipped us to succeed in His assignment. You need to be willing to make critical choices. If you are not willing to make the hard decisions, you'll never successfully fulfill God's assignment. The great news is once you make the tough decisions, God fills the void left behind with His grace and provision. His joy and blessing will follow you when you walk in your Godly assignment. God has a spectacular plan for you. You will be amazed at what God will do through you! Discover his assignment; make the right choices and watch your life soar! I do say this to you: don't do anything without praying about it, without knowing in your heart that it is from the Lord and no one else.

Chapter 9 –
The Awakening

How many times have you said to yourself, "It's time for me to wake up and fly right," because your life is going to hell in a hand basket, and you have not done anything to make it right. Every year is the same old thing, making new year's promises, telling the Lord what you are going to do, asking Him to get you out of this one, and if He does, you promise to do better and fly right. You promise to go to church and pray more. Let me ask you this question: when are you going to wake up and fly right? Did I get your attention? Did your mouth fly open, and did your eyes open wide? Did you start thinking about what it is I am saying to you? I want to be a woman who keeps it real, who keeps it "one hundred" all the times. We live in a sometimes fake world with sometimes fake people. What wakes you up and what motivates you to get up and push past your ups and downs? Who motivates you, if anyone or anything does? In this chapter, we will cover some things, maybe some ideals, but most of all the presence of the Lord. That's one thing that will awaken you. One thing that will keep you asleep would be things you cover up with false self, with false reasoning and unbelief. What I mean is the many times you tried to be something you are not meant to be, trying to be like your friends doing what they do. You even try to be the way you think your family wants you to be. Have you ever listened to your voice in your head saying, "Follow me; don't listen to other people; stop that mess." Wake up. Listen to your heart. Are you remembering who you are as a person? Can you do that for yourself? Is your time spent working, watching TV or trying to unwind from the cares of the day? There are things you must try, things you must build upon in order to have a solid emotional foundation in your life, and things that embrace your true nature of everything you come in contact with.

You have to believe God is the answer to your amazing life, so you must learn to live in the moment, and be grateful with what you have, where you are going, and who you are with. But first, you must learn how to wake up from all those dead dreams, from all those dead relationships. Wake up from all those "should've, would've, could've" sayings. The next time, it's going to be so different, and you are going to do better if you get another chance. Have you heard yourself saying this before?

Let's talk about some things you can do to boost your awakening process back to life. God has a plan for you, and you have life inside of you just waiting to fulfill His plan. All you need to do is tap into it, uncover it, build on it, and go from there with the strength of God.

Colossians 2:6-7: "As ye have therefore received Christ Jesus the Lord, so walk ye in him: Rooted and built up in him, and established in the faith, as ye have been taught, abounding therein with thanksgiving. So teach us to number our days, that we may apply our hearts unto wisdom. "And be not conformed to this world: but be ye transformed by the renewing of your mind that ye may prove what is good, and acceptable, and perfect, will of God."

This should teach you how to get your thoughts together and to pull yourself up and arise, because this is your awakening moment; it all starts here, so move.

TRANSPARENT PEOPLE

Are you a transparent person? By being transparent, how can you bring about a better life for yourself and others? Reveal what you want and don't want for your life and in your life; reveal these things are open not obvious Lead by example, help family and friends and your enemies do better. What I mean by leading by example is, don't just tell someone to act in a right way, show them and give them a taste of your good life, and allow them to walk in your footsteps as well. Have you ever planted seeds, or sowed seeds of righteousness and goodness into your family, into your own life and in the lives of others? Good seeds are needed to make good fruit, good fruit that God has planted, the fruit of life. At this time, you should be a force to be reckoned with; yes you, with your smart, transparent self.

What does all this mean to you? Have you ever found yourself in the wrong place in life? You leave that place and go right back to another wrong place in your life. Why do you stay there so long? You say this is your future, and you are done with the past, and this was one of the best years of your life. Could this mean you have moved between the walls of life and become bold enough to say it? Don't be a fake person. In the bible, Paul was not afraid to allow others to see him as he was. For those who don't understand what transparent means, allow me to give you a short meaning. It could mean a see-through person, a self-evident person, or even an easy to perceive person. Are you transparent enough that people have reason to trust you? Should we be transparent as Christians? Or do you have anything to hide? Just be to the point when you are transparent . Allow others to hear your story and this may encourage them. No one just came down from heaven riding on a cloud.

You should also be careful who you want to look like. There are so many different looking people in this world who look like sheep in wolves' clothing, doing all kind of wrong, saying whatever they want to say, and going just about everywhere doing wrong. If you don't think so, look around you and tell me what you see. Look in your city, your towns, even in your own neighborhoods. Talk to some people around there and see what they have to say about different things and see how their lives are going whether they need any help making it work. We are living in a world today full of hate and hateful people with so much disrespect in their hearts, so many dishonors for other people's lives. But most of all it's so chaotic, a state of complete confusion and disorder. Look at the news; there are so many people lost out there, just walking around like zombies with a blank look on their face, going nowhere and feeling useless about themselves. If we are not going to help, don't even start talking about them. I feel God has placed us here to help, to love, to let people know that there's a true and living God who is not dead but very much alive.

If you are going to focus on God, you should be able to see yourself as an everyday, God-loving person detecting the true nature of lies and deception because you can see through it. Don't you want the drive of it all? You have to stand out from the rest and live the transparent life. Can you describe something in your life that is so obviously true that there's no room for any questions or debate about it? I love the Lord because he has heard my cry and as long as I live and trouble arises, I will hasten to His thorn. Be bold enough to say, "I love Jesus." Be transparent enough to say, "I can do all things with Jesus' help." Be loving for the place where the Lord has you in, and where He's leading you to. Be caring for the peace He has you in, so at the end of the day, always say something to your heavenly father. Thank Him always.

THANK YOU, FATHER, FOR LOVING ME IN SPITE OF ALL MY SINS. YOU HAVE RESTORED MY BROKEN HEART, AND RESTORED MY MIND TO PEACE; YOU HAVE GIVEN ME A NEW WALK, AND

WITH EACH STEP I MAKE YOU ARE THERE. LOVE YOU, FATHER.

I must go on for those of you that are married or going to get married in the near future, but truly this is for everyone. I may not know much, but this is what I think about what transparent marriages are; this is to wake everyone up. There's more awakening happening here, but this one is called "transparent awakening."

Have you ever shared your dreams with your spouse? Have you ever just sat down and truly went there with each other? Are you open about your needs and wants? Do you think it matters? Are you honest about everything, or are you just given the normal. I won't be on this marriage subject too long because I am not experienced in it, but I know someone who is great with it: my Pastor and First lady. So tell me how you will define your relationship with your partner. Is it an open one or are you being guarded about some things? Maybe you are even being transparent about some things in your lives. I think that I will be marrying someone who makes me fall head-over-heels in love with God on a daily basis in my life; how about you?

Transparency itself should not be your primary goal in your marriage, Jesus should be. Don't you think being transparent should merely be how you seek the honor of knowing Jesus by obedience? By doing what He has asked you to do and not to do, or even being what He has called you to be in life? Love your partner better; love yourself better as well. You have to even live better. Someone told me that transparency is a great tool we use to honor God through right living, and know that there are always two sides to a coin and you must trust that one side is different. You must be trustworthy at all times. Don't let in sin or hurt because you are hurt or have a broken heart because you haven't allowed forgiveness in or prayed about anything. Don't let your bitterness turn into brokenness; you'd better start building trust up if you have lost it; you'd better repair that foundation because transparency has cracked that foundation, so you must allow the presence of the Lord to enter in and start repairing it.

Have you made poor financial choices, or hidden things from each other, or is it that old two-sided trust? All of this is called a transparent marriage. A happy marriage is good, but it's more about holiness than happiness. Is your marriage created by God or is it a one-man show or is it even an "into me" kind of love? You'd better ask God to build you back up. Mark 10: 6-9 says:

"But from the beginning of the creation God made them male and female.

For this cause shall a man leave his father and mother, and cleave to his wife;

And they twain shall be one flesh: so then they are no more twain, but one flesh. What therefore God hath joined together, let not man put asunder."

This is so true. If we can just get more families with both parents in the home, where there is love and peace, where there are fathers needed in the homes to raise up their sons and daughters — just maybe there would not be so much hateful men and women in this world who just want to fight back for their hurt and pain someone else caused. Just maybe home would not have to hurt when we go to bed or when our parents are talking to each other. We won't feel like they are in a bad place with each other and maybe in the next room fighting. I must say you never know whose home is not with peace. There may not even be any love there. How many of you grew up this way and became your mother or your father? You can look into the mirror and see them. You have allowed yourself to even act like them by hurting the ones you love. You were not too transparent then, were you? I am sorry. I just had to go there. This has taken me to another place in my life. I have seen many beautiful men and women die from killing each other from years of abuse, from years of telling each other I will kill you before I let you go. That kind of talk does it all the time. Or people who take their whole family out with them, kids and all. What has happened to the minds of these people? Has the devil entered in? Has life gotten to them so badly that they stop caring for themselves and others, or just stop praying? Maybe they didn't know God at all, or maybe they just didn't have anyone in their life to help them along the way. Are you so transparent that no one can see you to ask for help? Make yourself known to someone. Jesus would have.

Chapter 10 –
The Closing

The Closing: what goes through your mind when you hear those words? Well, throughout this chapter, we will explore the things God has closed, you have closed, or things you might need to close but haven't closed yet. Let's explore them together and find out what God has to say about it and more. First things first; throughout your life, doors were opened, things happened, people came and went in your life. The good, the bad and the ugly has happened in every area of your life, but have you truly closed any doors? Have you allowed the Lord to close some for you? God closed some doors; have you opened them back up? Can you sit back and remember what doors needed closing because you were going to lose your mind? This was the door of a broken heart. Remember that man or that woman who walked out on you, that child who broke your heart, that mother or father who wasn't there for you when you needed them. That relationship in which you were cheated on or just wasn't ready to be loved? That was a door that needed closing fast. God will close doors. You may have to send or enable someone else to go in your place, someone to check out the situation for you, or be your partner in enabling God's will to be done. It may be that you have the right plan, but you are the wrong person. It may be you are the right person, but God wants you to team up with someone to accomplish the task He has put before you. That's why He will close a door just for this reasoning. Are you in a ministry teaming up with someone so that God's work is not totally dependent on you alone? We are here to help others. Are you able to pass the ball to another team member in the open field just as you are about to be tackled? That's good offense in football and makes great sense in ministry, too.

Closed doors are often God's way of refining us, preparing us for the door He will eventually open. I feel that God's will is focused more on how we respond to the closed door. If we run from the "trial of waiting," we may miss God's will that is to be accomplished at the reopening of some of the doors He closed. Yes, God will open some doors when needed for His glory only. Satan's got a plot, but God's got a plan for your life; sometimes, your plans don't work out because God has better ones. Do you know how many times we say we are going to do things and never do them? Well, God has put our plans on the back burner, and that's where they are going to stay until He closes the chapter of that mess we call greatness. It's amazing how we think we are doing well when the only thing happening is a hot mess going in the wrong direction. Are you convinced God wants you to open that door He closed? I feel God closes doors to mess because, let's be truthful about it, we won't. I sat in my mess for years trying to make things work out on my own, my way, fixing this, fixing that, or trying to. I was so glad when the Lord closed all those doors of hate, worry, loneliness, and most of all blame, yes blame. Don't think everything you do, right or wrong, is the right thing for you from God, and don't think you won't stuffer for doing well. You know when you start blaming yourself for all the wrong in your life and for all the things people have done to you.

Let's start with hate. Wow, that is the word of all words. We hate the ones who did the most dirt to us. We hate people who didn't do anything to help when they knew that someone was hurting us and they knew it was wrong. Hate has a hurtful feeling behind it. That word is powerful and will cut you. In God's word, He said hate no one, just pray for them.

OPPORTUNITY

Doors of relationships and circumstances are closed fast without any questions; sometimes, closed doors can be a bit more challenging and so emotional. When an opportunity coming your way that you thought was going to come through becomes unavailable, you may even question God's goodness or His foreknowledge, but why would you? As if you knew what you were doing. When a relationship ends or comes to a screeching halt, what do you do about it? Do you start to feel discouraged or even hurt, maybe even frustrated? But was it what God put together, or was it straight from you? At times, God opens up doors of blessing in our lives, but we just need to be grateful about it and accept and receive. Have you been grateful about anything? Have you allowed God to open and close some doors in your life? Sometimes, you pray persistently for God to open a door for you, and then, when it opens, you need to have an open mind to the different means and methods by which God seeks to bless you and open doors for you. Let the Lord know that you love Him with every breath in your body, with every song that you sing. God is the beginning, the middle and the end of your life, and when you feel that you can't take it anymore, have faith and take it to the Lord.

Sometimes, God closes doors because it's time to move forward. He knows we won't move unless circumstances force us to. Let me share with you how circumstances will take a move of God to push you into where you should belong. Were you in fear of becoming who He wanted you to be or because you were truly afraid? Don't you know that fear is among one of the most debilitating sprits? It will paralyze your thoughts and your will to live. Have you ever heard this before? Mirror, mirror on the wall. What do you see when you look in it each day? Do you see the old you or do you see a "survival of the fittest" person with a physical, mental and beautiful personality. We all have to be more powerful at each age of our lives. I have found out as a woman personally that we are winners. And to those people who are trying to live Godly lives and do the right things in their hearts, minds and bodies by seeking each day His presence, we can never be too busy doing too much of nothing. God's given desires of our hearts and His kingdom and righteousness must live on in us. In Luke 12:23-24 are the promises of God. Read it for yourself; it will bless you real good. Also, read 1 Corinthians 2:9-10; this is where God lives.

Have you ever wondered or looked so often for so long and regretfully upon the closed door that you don't even see the ones God has opened for you? "Keep thy heart with all diligence; for out of it are the issues of life." (Proverb 4:23)

Have you read this? The heart has issues. That's why you are supposed to guard your heart; don't allow the issues of life in.

In Chapter 13, there are note pages for you to write down some doors that the Lord has closed for you, ones that you opened because you thought they shouldn't have been closed. Remember that God closed them. Write down the ones you opened back up after God closed them as well.

REMEMBER TO PRAY ABOUT EVERYTHING AND KEEP GOD CLOSE IN ALL YOU DO AND SAY!!!!

Chapter 11 –
Didn't I Blow Your Mind?

A MOVE OF GOD

In this chapter, you will find yourself seeking after God more, seeking after His presence more, seeking after more of His wisdom for your life. So what it's raining; it can still be beautiful. Seek the Lord in the rain; love Him in the rain, and let Him love you through it all. As the rain pours down on your life and things are not good, you will need shelter. God is here to catch every drop. Haven't you realized that God is in the mist of it all? No matter how much the rain comes down or how fast it hits the problems in your life, and no matter how much it hurts, no matter if you can't see Him or feel Him, and you can't see two feet in front of you, and the pain is too much—just fall down on your knees, cry out to him because it will take a move of God.

To the man or woman reading this, please listen up. I know you may be worried about something; you may even be struggling in some way or another. You may even be questioning God right now. So, listen up. God loves you, and He has a plan for you that will bring you out and bring you back to Him, your first love. You can't do this alone. Trust Him, and don't miss out on the blessing He has for you. Have you ever thought about just asking, seeking, even knocking on the door of God's heart? Read, Luke 11:9. "I will take my hand and guide you."

Don't think just because you have made a mistake and you can't see your way out, that there's no future for you. Stop thinking you won't ever get married or be able to have that big wedding because of your big bell. Yes, I said it. Big belly. Did you think that I forgot about that chapter? No, I just had so many things in between to talk about, but it all blends together. I know what you are thinking. Your girlfriends are telling you that you are crazy. That man got you pregnant, and you know he is not marrying you now. He is fine and all, but can I keep it real with you? Don't for once think that just because you were in an abusive situation, had some kids, dropped out school, had to find you and your children a place to live, that all those things don't matter because the do. Okay, you allowed him to have it before you guys were married; I am not saying this with an okay choice. But the deed is done and you must move on. Now, your friends and family are saying things like, "It was just him in the room in the dark and you weren't even there." Don't tell me you have sat around letting family and friends speak nonsense to you or even fill your head up with unhealthy talk. You'd better guard what you hear from people, and watch what you say to them as well. Everybody is not meant to know all your stuff.

Then, for men, you allow your boys to start bashing in your ear, saying, "You know she asked for it, begged you for it; she was weak." A man and a woman are going to do whatever they want to do. Everyone knows right from wrong at one point in their lives. Things happen, but if we allow God to fill us up with His presence and we stay prayed up, sometimes, things like this won't happen. But if we keep putting God on the back burner, saying, "we got this" and we don't, things like this and more will happen. Stop and ask yourself where you are going from here because when it rains it pours, doesn't it? Life won't just stop for you and your problems. I want to help you get free. I becamepregnant out of wedlock, yes, testing the waters. I just wanted to see if I still had it or not. I was single and alone, and the test came back saying that I should not have opened the package until my wedding night. I should have kept reading the package, closed until wedding night. It's better that way, plus I knew that God was going to strike me down or throw some lightening bolts at me, but instead, He let me stay in my mess. I was afraid to allow Him in; the father who had a part in this did not have much to say. Is that how it goes? I never meant for this to happen. Isn't that something we always say? I couldn't do or say anything. I just started praying. Prayer always changes things in any situation.

This is what I think: how you walk with the broken is more important than how you sit with the greatest of them all. You don't have to pretend life doesn't hurt and people won't act the way you want them to or give you what you want. They aren't supposed to. That's the Lord's doing, and yours. People out there have to be doers and not let others do for them. Your expectation has everything to do with the level on which you receive things in life because your promise is attached to your assignment in life. So once you know what that is, whoops, there it is, the promise from God. God promises to forgive you when you ask Him to and mean it in your heart. Look up some of the promises God talks about in His word. Highlight them, remember them and hang on to His unchanging hands as my mother used to say to me. God's word never changes, and He never lies. You must stay on your God-given path and trust Him even when you are hurting, even when things don't seem like they are getting better; still trust Him, and give God your best always. You may have gotten off the path and onto a crooked road. So what?!! Find your way back. Push hard like never before. But first, you have to do some praying and some more praying; you need to get alone in your prayer closet with God and allow Him to talk to you, love on you, so you can feel His love and His peace in your heart and spirit.

Let's see what the bible has to say about all of this. In Proverbs 3:5-6 it says, "Trust in the Lord with all thine heart; and lean not unto thine own understanding and

In all thy ways acknowledge him, and he shall

direct thy paths." Then, in Proverbs 30:5 it also says, "every word of God is pure: he is a shield unto them that put their trust in him." John 14:1: "Let not your heart be troubled: ye believe in God, believe also in me."

John 14:2: "in my Father's house are many mansions: if it were not so, I would have told you, I go to prepare a place for you."

Read these passages and you will feel better about what's going on. Sometime, we have too much free time on our hands and we should be out there helping someone or getting involved in church.

Are you willing to get attached to something in life? Or maybe you can put your God-given talents to work and help someone get into ministry, sing a song, sweep a floor for your church. Just help someone with something; attach yourself to a dream, an ideal, a vision or even your children, who in this day and time need help just to live in this world. I have seen my fair share of hurting children. I figure if you can bring them into this world without the blessing of God, then you can at least give them a fighting chance to allow the breath of life to enter in their little bodies.

Remember that your struggles would be someone else's blessing. And life would be much easier to manage if you viewed it differently, such as an opportunity and not an obstacle. Sometimes, God closes doors in our lives because it's time to move forward. He knows we won't move unless circumstances force us to. Or things will get so hard and unsafe even to the point where you won't understand what's going on. Let me share with you how circumstances will take a move of God to push you into where you should belong. God has a reason for allowing things to happen. We may never understand His wisdom, but we simply have to trust His will. In Psalm 37:5 it says, "Commit thy way unto the Lord; trust also in Him; and He shall bring it to pass." In Matthew 19:26, with God all things are possible.

You can't even imagine how possible things could be if you would just let go and let God do the things He does so well, love on you. He has chosen you. He will bless you. Have you ever read Ephesians 1:3? It says "Blessed be the God and Father of our Lord Jesus Christ, who hath blessed us with all spiritual blessings in heavenly places in Christ." In Ephesians 1:5: "He also has predestined you, having predestinated us unto the adoption of children by Jesus Christ to himself, according to the good pleasure of his will." God also has redeemed you as well in Ephesians 1:17: "That the God of our Lord Jesus Christ, the Father of glory, may give unto you the spirit of wisdom and revelation in the knowledge of him." Then there's Ephesians 1:13: "He sealed you, In whom ye also trusted, after that ye heard the word of truth, the gospel of your salvation: in whom also after that ye believed, ye were sealed with that holy Spirit of promise." Take all of this and run with it, feel it, breathe it in and tell someone about it, don't keep it to yourself. Take what you learned and share it. Do what Jesus would do; learn from the best," Jesus." Read about Him.

Chapter 12 –
Knowing Your Worth

D o you know how much you are worth? If not, let's talk about it; you will never know how strong you are until being strong is your only way of choice. God is already there, so don't give up; it's going to happen. If God is for you, who can be against you? Know your worth; know that you are worthy to God, and He loves you very much. Give your entire attention to what God is doing right now in your life. Make yourself aware of it, and don't minimize that for one moment. Do you sometimes feel like you are worthless? Or, at times, have you been slighted or treated as though you were of little value? God cares for you so much! In fact, not even one sparrow dies and falls on the ground without God noticing it. I know you think that sparrows seem so small and worthless, but nothing in God's eyes is worthless, so get in His face and smile.

If God values the birds so much, how much does He care for and value you? Are you not more valuable than the birds? Yes! In fact, God knows so much about you that even every hair on your head is numbered. Wow! One soul is worth more than the entire world; for one soul, Jesus would have passed through the agony of Calvary so that one might be saved. God says that He will make you and me more precious than gold! And, when we look at the greatness of the price paid to save us, it was much more precious than gold! That's how much Jesus loves us! Think about how Jesus, the great and powerful Creator of our life, became a man and walked among us and then was crucified. And He did it because he loved and valued us so much that He wanted to save us from our sins! So we are of far greater value than anything in this world? The worth of a human soul can be estimated only by the light reflected from the cross of Calvary. Don't you think so? Let's remember how much we are of value in God's eyes! Remember to be nice and caring, but most of all, loving to all. It may be hard sometimes, but do it because of what Jesus has done for us and the great worth He has placed in our hearts. How do all the treasures and the glories, and all the worth of this world ever sink into insignificance when compared with the value of a human soul? Tell me how?

Don't get worked up about what may or may not happen tomorrow. You just don't know. GOD will help you deal with whatever hard thing comes up when the time comes. As we enter the close of this chapter, think about what knowing your worth means to you. Don't just sit there thinking you are not worth anything and no one cares about you or what goes on in your life. First, you have to care about who you are and how much you are worth to yourself. I know all your life people have talked about what they have or do not have, what they can get, who loves them, and where they have been in this world. You know, the whole nine yards. Don't think you are not worthy of the same things other people have and more. Knowing your worth, knowing your value, is not based on what others say about you; it's what you say about yourself. Life is too short even to allow wasted time on what others think or say about you. What does God say about you? Have you looked into the mirror? What do you see? If people had better things going on in their lives, you would not be the conversation piece in their homes. Stop comparing yourself to other people. None of us are alike; thank God for that one. Sometimes, we can be our own worst enemy; you must realize the key to happiness was never about things. God gave you value, He injected His confidence in you, and He affirmed you with His love. Don't you minimize that.

This is what the bible has to say about the matter: "For I know the thoughts that I think toward you, said the LORD, thoughts of peace, and not of evil, to give you an expected end." Jeremiah 29:11. "And be not conformed to this world: but be transformed by the renewing of your mind that ye may prove what is good, and acceptable, and perfect, will of God." (Romans 12, 2 2), Now, let's talk about being obedient to God.

Will obedience lead you to your first storm? Jesus doesn't give you immunity from any troubles in this world. He said in His word that we will have trials and tribulations; believe that one. Being obedient will give you an opportunity to see Jesus in the midst of your troubles. It's your choice if you want Jesus to join your troubles. Or do you want to go through the storm alone? So what is it going to be? Have you opened your eyes wide yet? Have you ever walked a path that took you straight out of yourself, and when you thought all was lost, your eyes opened to the fact that it is time to be obedient to God and allow Him to step in? You should thank God for protecting you from what you thought you wanted and blessing you with what you didn't know you needed. To that man out there who thought he had it all together, you thought that the world was about to come to an end just because you did the deed. Remember this: there's a God that understands. He may not like it, but He understands. He saw this coming before you cut the lights off. He tried to block it, but you did not hear it for the loud music, plus you didn't want to hear it or see the warning signs. He even made that special song skip a beat; He made the lights go on and off. With all of that going on, you both just weren't paying any attention to the signs. I know that all too well. Been there, done that.

Throughout this book, I have been talking to the ladies and a little to the men, but I care the same. I have been talking to anyone who was listening and willing to be set free. God's grace is here, His peace is here and so is His love for each and every one of you. Never let a problem that you may or may not be having get in the way of your love, peace and understanding for God because His timing is always perfect. So, if you don't know anything else, know this: you are worth more than you would ever dream. You just need to recharge your batteries because your desire to change is greater than your desire to stay the same. So, say to yourself out loud, "I am who I am, and no one's approval is needed or wanted." Your desire to change must be greater than your desire to stay the same always, so is your desire to change strong? Let's see.

In Chapter 13, you will have the opportunity to write down all your desires and the changes you had to go through to get there on the note pages.

YOU ARE AMAZING.

"Wow, weren't those last couple of chapters powerful and very informative? Did they have you sitting on the edge of your seat thinking? That's okay. Think about it; take it all in, and let the presence of the Lord enter in. Right now, I would like to get into the amazing part of it all, which you are. This is for all the strong men and women out there who are single and raising children and have heard some things, seen some things and have felt pain as well. To the young ones who are going through some things and have no one to tell. To the afraid, beaten, battered, and lost ones out there, Jesus loves you, and He is right there with you every step of the way. He said that you are amazing and wonderfully made. I can't sugar coat this for you so your feelings won't be hurt. Someone out there needs to hear this 100%. We have single dads out there as well. What about them? They didn't want to become fathers and raise children. Men have goals and visions to on what they would like for their families. Things happen true enough. Don't sit and act like they don't. We just don't want to talk about it, let alone hear about it. God said that you are amazing, beautiful and strong; take His word for it. When we get ourselves into different situations, we begin to feel sorry for ourselves. We begin to take things out on other people and on the ones who are trying to help us. Don't get it twisted; God made you and He knows your beginning and your ending, so don't sit and wholly in it, and please don't allow it to consume you. God will never leave you. I know what you are thinking: what planet is this lady living on because it's more than ups and downs. You say you have been through more than ups and downs. Would you call it pure hell? Sorry for keeping it so real. One hundred percent realness. Shoot, that wasn't a walk in the park. God had to truly work on you. I bet you were not feeling so amazing like Wonder Woman and superman at that time. Milk, bottles, pampers, up late, not enough sleep, hurting, not knowing what to do at times. How do you put your sweet children to bed when you are in so much pain? Buying clothes with money you don't have, walking them to school. I know there are some things I left out. Oh!! On top of all that, you were going through the worst thing in your life: abuse. Some of you can relate to that. God can put His super on your nature and His love on top of all your pain. This is why you are so amazing and wonderfully made in God's eyes; allow me to spell this out for you. Don't ever let anyone say to you that you are not an amazing person. Tell them God made you wonderfully from head to toe, and he doesn't make junk. He only makes amazing, beautiful people.

AMAZING means this to me and more:

A- I am the apple of my children's eyes.

M- You manage it all well with God's help.

A- You never leave them alone.

Z- Zealous, you are a passionate person, dedicated, strong and supportive.

I- The idea of it all doesn't scare you one bit; you got this.

N- Never without love, twenty-four-seven.

G- God is in everything you do and say, from top to bottom. You will instill love, peace, and joy in your children and love on them like never before.

I just left someone's mouth wide open, with your breathtaking, energetic, supportive self. Now go out there with your head high, chest out, standing tall; put on a smile and keep doing the best job God has given you to do and you will be okay. He promised you that.

Chapter 13 –
"HUSH," GOD IS TALKING

I want you to stop and talk to your heavenly father. Talk to him about whatever you need him to know. He knows anyway. See yourself sitting on his lap putting your arms around him and whispering all your cares to him. Don't hold back. Let it out. Free yourself because throughout this book he has been talking with you. Have you been listening?

Don't carry any of your mistakes around with you. Instead of carrying them, place them under your feet and use them as a stepping stone to rise above them, rise above whatever you've been though. Your story is the key that will unlock someone else's prison. You never know what kind of prison someone else has been in. Share your testimony with someone; put yourself out there and give a little. Let me ask you this question: what do you do when God is silent? Do you get frustrated? When God is so silent, it's easy for doubt to set in, isn't it? But just remember, silence is the most precious time of all; it allows you to sit back and pray about all the things you have inside of you. You have to stop, drop and give it to the Lord. So in these next few pages, get with your father and tell it all because you just went for the ride of your life, and you need to rest now and let God love on your mind and your body. You need to ask the Lord whatever He's doing in this season, please don't do it without you. Say, "Lord, if you are healing in this season, don't do it without me." So get your blessing; get whatever the Lord has for you. Don't ask for the things the devil took because if God allowed the devil to take those things from you, He has better things in store.

Before I close, I would like to share one more thing with you, one more very important thing. A feeling of anger or displeasure about someone or something unfair. Like I said before, don't carry hurt, pain or anything that would keep you from getting God's full attention for the walk in your life. Yes, I know that a lot has happened, you have been hurt and your children have felt some kind of way, maybe even hurt. Please don't allow bitterness to cloud your mind to your future for the kingdom of God; that's all that matters. I know it hurts, and sometimes you just want to scream out, so do that. God hears everything. He knows your heart and what's on your mind. So having a strong and often unpleasant flavor that is the opposite of sweet, a bitter taste in your mouth, how does that feel? You don't need to walk around bitter; that will cause painful emotions felt or experienced in a strong and unpleasant way, like being angrier and being unhappy because of the unfair treatment you have experienced in your life. After all the things that happened to me, I just wanted to be left alone. I know this is the time to talk to my heavenly father, but someone out there needs to hear the truth; bitter taste or not, this is real. In Romans 12:2 it says, "and be not conformed to this world: but be transformed by the renewing of your mind that ye may prove what [is] that good, and acceptable, and perfect, will of God." Then, there's one more thing; it's called:

Forgiveness, the act of forgiving someone or something, the attitude of someone who is willing to forgive other people. Are you willing to forget and forgive people, or are you still holding on to some things that will keep you from getting blessed by God? I would like to thank you for allowing me into your world and into your head. I pray that this book has blessed someone. I pray that God has entered the picture of your story and filled you up with His presence. I pray that you have allowed the presence of God to come down your street, into your work place, and into you.

What is forgiveness?

Forgiveness: Is it letting go of grudges and bitterness? Is it letting go of all the hurt and pain someone or something put on you or in you?

When someone you care about hurts you, do you hold on to it? Or do you allow resentment to set in and manifest inside of you, eating at your every thought, your every sense of who you are? You know this could lead to an act of revenge — so embrace forgiveness and move on from the pain of what was to what is about to be.

Nearly everyone has been hurt by the actions or words of another person. Perhaps it was your mother criticizing your parenting skills, how you act with your own kids, or even how you act with your mate. Your colleagues will sabotage a project of yours. Even your partner who you loved may have had an affair with someone you knew. These wounds can leave you with lasting feelings of anger, bitterness or even vengeance in your heart.

But if you don't practice forgiveness, you might be the one who pays the most deadly price. By embracing your forgiveness, you can also embrace peace, hope, gratitude and joy. You can even get the feeling of love back that someone took from you. Considering how forgiveness can lead you down the path of physical, emotional and spiritual well-being, you have to, you must allow the presence of the Holy Spirit to fill you with God's presence. Now, let's talk about forgiveness.

Generally, forgiveness is a decision to let go of resentment and thoughts of revenge. The act that hurt or offended you might always remain a part of your life, but forgiveness can lessen its grip on you and help you focus on others. Can you do that? Focus on the things you need to make happen and bring back the luster in your life to give you more positive parts of your life. Forgiveness can even lead to feelings of empathy and compassion for the one who hurt you.

Forgiveness doesn't mean that you deny the other person's feelings or responsibility for hurting you, and it doesn't minimize or justify the wrong that they have done. You can forgive the person without excusing the act, can't you? Forgiveness brings a kind of peace that helps you go on with your life. Please don't minimize this; you can go on. What are the benefits of forgiving someone?

Letting go of grudges and bitterness can make way for happiness, health, peace, and love. Forgiveness can lead to:

Healthier relationships with other people and your family

Greater spiritual and psychological well-being

Less anxiety, stress and hostility will allow you to have a straight face when talking or acting with others

1. Will lower your blood pressure
2. Lesser symptoms of depression
3. Your immune system will be stronger
4. Improvement of your heart health and your self-esteem will be healthier

Why is it so easy to hold a grudge?

How do you reach a state of forgiveness? Move away from your role as victim and release the control and power the offending person and situation have had in your life; release it to God. He is the only one who can fix it. I would like for you to dig deep into your mind and remember all the things that you needed to tell the Lord, no matter what it is Only you and God will ever know. This is a little biblical story of Jacob and Esau; it should be familiar to most bible readers; if not, please read the story in Genesis. Jacob and Esau were the sons of Isaac. Esau, as the elder son, stood to receive the firstborn's share of the inheritance from Isaac. Jacob, aided by his mother, used a tremendous amount of deceit in order to steal this birthright inheritance from his brother, in Genesis 27.

What Jacob did was not a small thing. It was not as though he had borrowed something from his brother and neglected to return it. This inheritance would give Jacob the best things in life, including mastery over his brother Esau (Genesis 27:28-29). Esau's reaction to what Jacob had done was nothing less than bitter rage.

Jacob was in no doubt a wealthy man and he could afford to offer presents beyond the means of most of us. The value of the gifts, however, was not the important thing in this situation. The important thing was Jacob's humility and his willingness to be the peacemaker. This was just a little bible story that you will find in the Genesis 27. Read it; it will bless you.

What can we learn about overcoming grudges?

We have to be willing to take the lead in reconciliation, swallowing our pride and holding our temper when needed. We have to overcome our grudges and desire for revenge and be willing to offer the gifts of peace. This will not always guarantee forgiveness and a healed relationship, but the biblical instructions we have seen tell us that we must be willing to try at least! Because forgiving is a gift each one of us can give to another.

Chapter 14

FINAL THOUGHTS

I know that life has touched you in one way or another, and it left you with a bitter taste in your mouth. It also left you with a broken heart. Your head doesn't work, so you can't think straight, and fear of the unknown fills your every thought. Did you know fear will limit you and your vision? But your self-worth can serve you better when you can empower yourself to walk down an even street, a brighter street, a well-lit path. You must find what's more important to your spirit—your past or your God-given future.

Ask yourself, where do you go from here? Don't allow what you've been though to affect your beautiful life God has given you. If you have seen too much, been through some hard times, didn't know which way to turn, and you thought God had left you, think again. God has been there with you the whole time. He has been closer like your dreams; that's close. God wants you to be healthy in mind, body and spirit. Let's talk about a few things to help you get through all your hurt and pain, all your "I didn't know what to do" stuff, and through all your "I am alone" fears. Let's go through some deadly things that can hurt you, in PROVERBS 11:2.

"When pride cometh, then cometh shame; but with the lowly is wisdom."

PROVERBS 29:23

"A man's pride shall bring him low: but honor shall uphold the humble in the spirit."

We all struggle with pride at one point in our lives. Some of us don't even realize it because we have struggled with it so long and without some kind of help. Yes!! Help. There is help for everything in this world. Your way or God's way, but you must let go either way of your pride and move on forward with God.

Allow me to explain what pride is first. I'm not a spiritual doctor, but I do know Jesus, and He has allowed me to help in the way that I know how, so listen up, please.

PRIDE: "the state or feeling of being proud, becoming or dignified sense of what is due to oneself or one's position or character; self-respect; self-esteem." It can also mean this: "pleasure or satisfaction taken in something done by or belonging to oneself or believed to reflect credit upon oneself." You know, self-worth. The bible says it's one of the deadly sins.

PSALM 10:4

It explains that the proud are so consumed with

themselves that their thoughts are far from God." The wicked through the pride of his countenance, will not seek after God and is not in all His thoughts. This kind of haughty pride is the opposite of the spirit of humility that God seeks.

MATTHEW 5:3

"Blessed are the poor in spirit, for theirs is the kingdom of heaven." The poor in spirit are those who recognize the utter spiritual inability to come to God aside from His grace. The proud, on the other hand, are so blinded by their pride they think they have no need for God in their lives, or even worse, God should accept them for who they are just because they deserve His acceptance. How do you feel about that? Is this you in any sense of the word? If so run, and run fast! Pride goes before destruction and a haughty spirit before a fall. It's better to be lowly in spirit than to share the blunder.

Now here's how you saw yourself through these pages, and you need to talk to someone. Know that help is always around the corner. So you'd better start owning who you are as God's child, and stop having all those pity parties with yourself because you are a true Marathon Runner. You just ran a life-changing run on all kinds of bumpy roads and came out a winner. Praise God; His love never failed you. To the proud: wasn't Satan cast out of heaven because of his pride? ISAIAH 14:12-15 will tell you about it. What we say about ourselves means nothing in God's work; it's what God says about us that makes the whole difference.

Now, let's talk about why is pride so sinful. PRIDE

is giving ourselves the credit for something that God has accomplished for us. PRIDE is taking the glory that belongs to God and keeping it for ourselves. But anything we have accomplished in this old world would not be possible if it was not for God enabling and sustaining us. Tell me, what do you have that you think you received on your own, and if you did receive it, why boast like you didn't receive anything at all from God? You'd better check yourself, and watch out for PRIDE. It's a natural born killer. Here are some more spiritual guidelines to help you understand the meaning of pride and why you have to clean it up out of your life. I pray this was a blessing to you and started you on your way to a healthier you, and to focus more on Jesus. He is our ultimate example of selflessness. Read these scriptures for understanding and help.

JAMES 4: 6 AND 10
PHILIPPIANS 2: 3
ROMANS 12: 3 AND 16
1 CORINTHIAN 13: 4
JEREMIAH 9:23

FINALE. No, I don't think so. there's more to be said, so listen up. I will give you some insight on how to get from where you are now to where you need to be. You can't get there alone and that's for sure, so let's begin. First you need a makeover—you know, like a "do it over"—but this will be from God. He will be your makeup artist. The first thing He does is to make sure you are out of His way by standing clear from the edges because you are about to go through the protected wash, where you get washed with the blood of Jesus and get a very special under coating — a healthy, protected coating of His love, more peace, more joy and His wisdom. Then, you must take care of all your unresolved anger which you know you have. God is about to put you under surveillance, watching to see if there's anything preventing you from moving on to getting healthy.

Now, let's get to that anger. What is anger first of all? Anger sometimes serves a purpose; it releases deeper issues and problems like internal conflicts. It's better to release anger than to turn it around to destroy oneself. The key to understanding anger is not to suppress it. Don't hold it in, and don't release it as pain, but release it as acceptance by taking a deep breath; exhale it. Release that anger into the world. Give it back to where it came from, one's past and all the things bad within. Don't allow anger to linger around; move on it quickly because anger will chip away at you if you let it. Do this for yourself and no one else. You will come out like new money. Trust and believe the power of God.

Notes pages...Write Away